SHOWIN' YA THE ROPES

A YOUNG ADULT'S RESOURCE GUIDE TO NAVIGATE LIFE

John Eyres

PUBLISHING

Kenzie Publishing
St. Louis, MO

Kenzie Publishing
12713 Willowyck Dr.
St. Louis, MO 63146
John@ShowinYaTheRopes.com

www.ShowinYaTheRopes.com

ORDERING INFORMATION
Quantity sales, individual sales, special discounts are available on quantity purchases by corporations, associations, schools, and others. For details, contact the publisher at the address above.

Copy editing by Jerry Abernathy

Cover Design & Book Design by Compelling Communications, Inc. (compelcom.com)

ISBN 0-9769762-3-4

FIRST EDITION

10 9 8 7 6 5 4 3 2

Table of Contents

Dedication

I dedicate this book to my wife Kristine Eyres,
who is my best friend, and has always been so kind
and loving and supportive to me. I also dedicate
this book to my loving children;
Whitney, Blake, Mckenzie and Gabrielle,
who so unselfishly allowed dad to take the
many hours away from them to write this book.

I also want to honor my parents,
Florence and Wesley Eyres,
who taught me strong moral values,
how to have a good work ethic,
raised me in a Christian home with love,
kindness and strong discipline.
Most of all I thank my mother for instilling in me
the value and importance of setting goals in life.

Acknowledgments

As with any large project, including writing a book, there are friends and business associates that I called upon for their expertise in reviewing the specific chapters of my book. Without their helpful comments, suggestions, and critiques the book would have certainly missed specific areas of interest in which they guided me on by having their helpful review.

In gratitude and admiration I want to thank the following people:

William Beaman, M.D.
    Creve Coeur Primary Care Group, St. Louis, Missouri

Mike Novak, Partner
    Alternative Mortgage Solutions, Crestwood, Missouri

David and Nicole Crank Jr.
    Pastor and wife, Faith Christian Ministries, Fenton, Missouri

John Simon, Owner and Mark R. Moore, Jr, Escrow Closer
    Archway Title Agency, Inc., St. Louis, Missouri

Dave S. Walsh, AAI
    Walsh Financial Services, Creve Coeur, Missouri

Nick Schneider, CFP, ChFC, CLU
    Mass Mutual Financial Group, Chesterfield, Missouri

Phil Miceli, Registered Representative
    Mass Mutual Financial Group, Chesterfield, Missouri

John S. Korte, FLMI, AIRC, Manager, Life & Health Section
    Missouri Department of Insurance, Jefferson City, Missouri

June Van Klaveren, President
    Compelling Communications Inc., Manchester, Missouri

Donna Johnson, Real Estate Agent
    RE Max Suburban Realtors, Chesterfield, Missouri

Mike Weeks, Attorney
    Rudy D. Beck & Associates, St. Charles, Missouri

Terry Musclow, Sales Representative
    Dickinson Press Inc., Grand Rapids, Michigan

Jerry B. Abernathy, Editor
    Educational and Publishing Services, St. Louis, Missouri

INTRODUCTION

The future is wide open for the taking. You have your whole life ahead of you. Life can be exactly what you make it to be. These are just a few of the quotes passed on from your parents, grandparents and friends as you graduate High School or College. This book was written as a resource guide to help young adults understand some of the most important building blocks as they progress into Adulthood. It is a book written in the pretense of something I wish I could have grabbed onto earlier in life versus later. The culture today for the X generation is cellphones with Internet messaging, wearing enough "bling-bling" to show how cool I am, body piercing and tattooing, short skirts and tops to show some skin, untucked shirts and baggy pants, highlighted hair, me first, myself, and it's all about **ME**!

But you have a long way to go to get to where you want to be, right? One of my favorite tunes from The Little River Band is *It's A Long Way There*. That song tells the story of it's a long way there to get to where you're going. This book can help you get there.

Each chapter has a focus on some basic building blocks to give you information about some things you probably don't have a clue about. It shares wisdom and knowledge on subjects that are important to you for becoming more successful. If I had applied the principals outlined in the chapters, I would definitely have gone farther and faster, than the slow paced ride I have taken the past 25 years.

This book was built to help you succeed in areas you know very little about. Insight in to subjects you have not been taught in school that deal with life's greatest issues, which can make or break you. Why not take the easier road. Take the time to **READ** this book and learn about the content. If you apply what you learn, amazing things will begin to happen.

It's all about **YOU**! Reference any particular chapter as you enter your life's journey and be ready for the positive changes down the road that will meet up with you.

You want to be successful, but you don't know all the answers. Let's face it, nobody has all the "yes" answers to life. In **Showin' Ya The Ropes** you will get an overlook how to:

- Choose the right career/profession/business.
- Set goals in life and grasp why goal setting is so important.

- Create a simple budget plan.
- Establish good credit history and how it affects your future.
- Buy your first house and develop knowledge of the process.
- Start your financial planning early in life so it really pays off for you later in life.
- Understand all about insurance in protecting what you own and using wills.
- Think outside of the box by diversifying your income potential.

In all of these areas you will find easy to read and practical suggestions to help you make better decisions as you build your life, your lifestyle and the road you want to travel.

The building blocks below can help you construct a stronger foundation as you grow into adulthood.

So...letz get gon...seeulatr...fyi!

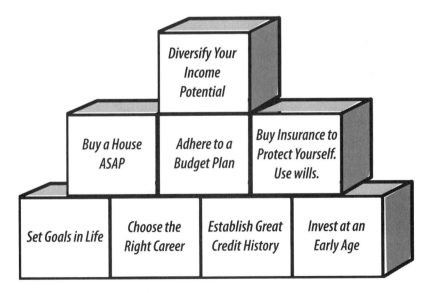

1

CHOOSING A CAREER, PROFESSION OR BUSINESS

Decide Now to Plan Your Job Pathway for Life

Young people, now is the time to decide and plan for your future. What is it you want out of your life? Is it a good paying job or a big family, do you want to travel and see other regions of the country? Do you want to get married or do you see yourself single for most of your life? Do you want to live in a big house with a wrap around front porch, or can you see yourself living in a huge loft condo in the city? Do you prefer country living or city living? What about getting married and raising a family, do you want children or do you just want pets?

In this chapter I hope to set a ground flight pattern in your early years after you graduate High School. These are some of the most important years in your young adult stage, as I believe they will form some key building blocks as to where you climb in your life's mountain of adventure. Whether you have a plan of attack or not will make a big difference as to your success as a person, a husband or wife, an employee or even a good friend to others. This book is geared to be a guideline to help you make some very important decisions in some key destinations for your life in the years ahead. In moving forward let's begin with **YOU**. It's your future, what are you planning to do with it?

> *Words of Wisdom: The harder you work at bettering yourself in your 20's the more it should pay off for later in life!*

Going to college, finishing a graduate degree, working longer hours at your job, working 2 jobs, saving money to buy a house – whatever it takes, push yourself young to enjoy yourself old.

As you enter into young adulthood and graduate from High School, I believe it is crucial that you as an individual take some "time-outs" to think about your life ahead of you. Find a quiet place to be alone, whether it's your bedroom or a picnic table at the park, choose your setting carefully so you are not bothered and have a peaceful mode of think time. I suggest 6-7 "time-outs" across a 2-month period to build your very own database of who, why, how and what makes you tick. Take a notebook to write down your thoughts, goals and answers as you build your database.

Time-Out #1 Write down 25 answers to these questions: What makes you happy, what are some of the best experiences in the past 18-20 years that you have enjoyed? Was it a special relationship with a friend or a pet? Was it a camping trip to Colorado or a beach trip with your family to Florida? Was it a summer camp experience or a canoe trip? Did you like playing sports on a team in High School; was it a blast in your theater class or what about cooking in home economics? Was it a visit to your aunt or uncle's house where they have a tractor and a garden that takes up most of their day? Do you like playing a musical instrument in the band or orchestra? Was it a field trip to the history museum that really caught your interest? Do you like working around the house fixing things? Do you like working on your car? Do you like sewing your own clothes? The goal here is to try to find out what it is you enjoy about life, what you like doing, what makes you feel good.

Time-Out #2 Write down 7-10 career paths you have been thinking about that you would like to do in your life: Take some quiet time to think about this. Do you want to be a teacher and help kids, do you want to be a fireman or a policeman, do you want to own your own business, do you want to work with people who are sick? What is it that you think you could be good at and would find your success whether it would be working at a Ford Plant, installing lawn sprinkler systems, being a nurse or doctor, a lawyer or business sales person? Try to be specific with the area you are thinking about. For instance if you want to be a doctor narrow the field. What kind of doctor? Maybe a pediatrician, general practitioner, surgeon or cancer specialist. Don't be afraid to think outside of the box, be realistic but I encourage you to be a dreamer, too. Make your list and go over it a couple of times.

Time-Out #3 Write down a list of 25 things you want to achieve in your life. A list of goals that you believe you can achieve. This list can be anything from buying a brand new Corvette to purchasing a full-length fur coat. Do you want a large 2-story house or would you be content with a ranch house in the country on 3 acres of land? Do you want to travel abroad, see other countries and meet people of foreign culture? Would you want to live in Colorado in the mountains and then live in California on the beach and finally end up living on a lake in Minnesota? Do you plan to get married, have a family, how many kids do you want? Do you have aspirations to go into politics and be the Governor of Missouri or President of the United States?

Time-Out # 4 In this quiet time session I want you to combine and cross check Time-Out # 2 and Time-Out # 3. For example:

Career Path	Goal
Teacher (Teachers have 2 months off in the summer & this would allow you to travel.)	I like working with kids, I want to be at home with my family in the summertime. I want to travel more.
Pediatrician (Pediatricians treat children, make good money & control their own work schedule.)	I like working with children. I want a big house & a large family. I want a BMW & control of my work week
Mechanic (They like working with cars, tools, and driving all kinds of autos.)	I like working around cars. I want a Corvette some day.
Carpenter (Craftsmen who like working with tools, not confined to a desk job, enjoy finishing a project.)	I like to build things. I want to work outside. I want to build my own house some day. I'm good with tools.

Career Path	Goal
Dental Hygienist (They work with all kinds of people, make good money, have decisions over how many days they want to work.)	I want to be in the healthcare field. I want to have a flexible work schedule & be able to stay at home when my children are young.
Salesperson (They have a flexible schedule, in & out of the office, with a commission program, they can earn unlimited money.)	I want to work with a lot of different people. I like to travel, not be confined to an office. I want to be paid based on how hard I work.

Note: It takes money to achieve certain goals and desires!

Time-Out # 5 In this session take 30-60 minutes to fine tune your "individual" setting for what could be a career direction for you. Write down on paper and assemble your database information specifically mapped to your needs, wants and desires. You need to spend some serious "think time" studying your compiled written job mapping calculations. Try to narrow your job/career goals down to 3-5 job professions you **BELIEVE** sincerely could be a fit for you. Write them down. Now seek out people from those professions to go talk to.
Ask your parents, friends teachers, counselors, aunts and uncles, to help you identify a person to contact in the 3-5 career areas you have chosen. Compose a list with the referral name, their phone number, address where they work and then either contact that person by phone or write them a letter explaining the process you have done and ask them for a meeting to discuss/share their chosen job career with you.
Time-Out # 6 Write down 20-30 questions to ask the people you interview concerning your career choices. The more questions you come up with the more information you will gather. Here are some questions to get you started:
1. Why did you choose this job/career path?
2. How many years of college/schooling does your profession require?
3. Was the pain worth the gain?
4. What do you like most about your job?

5. What do you like least about your job?
6. Could you share a typical workday with me, from morning to evening?
7. What kind of clothes do you wear for your job?
8. Is traveling (the time spent in the car to work) a concern for you?
9. In this job how is it working with other people at your office?
10. Are you happy with the money you are making with this job?

Now set up your meeting times with the people you contacted. Ask them if you can possibly spend part of the day with them, experiencing their daily "job." Make sure you talk to a couple people in the area you are looking to make as a career. The more information you have, the more successful you will be and the more educated you become.

Compile the information you have put together, including the responses from the job career person you interviewed and try to lay out a plan for your future. What is a good direction for you to take? Make sure to sit down with your parents and share the strategic mapping career program with them and ask for their input. Now give it your best effort to come up with a chosen career path that fits you.

Still undecided? Let's look at possible careers that can help clear the picture.

Looking at ALL the POSSIBILITIES

I encourage everyone who reads this book, especially the first chapter, to take a serious look at a college education. You can reap a lot of benefits by having a solid education and the opportunity to make more money climbs higher with an education. But...college is not for everyone, so take your time and spend your hours wisely looking at all the possibilities.

> *Words of Wisdom: Your attitude determines your altitude!*

Colleges and Universities

Barnes-Jewish Hospital College

	314-454-7055	(jhconah.edu)
Brooks Bible Institute	314-773-0083	(brooksbibleinstitute.org)
Belleville Area College	314-436-3218	(swic.edu)
Central Methodist College	636-305-1007	(centralmethodist.edu)
Columbia College	314-429-5500	(ccis.edu)

Covenant Theological Seminary
          314-434-4044   (covenantseminary.edu)
Deaconess College of Nursing
          314-768-3044   (deaconess.edu)
Eden Theological Seminary 314-961-3627   (eden.edu)
Fontbonne University   314-889-1400   (fontbonne.edu)
Harris-Stowe College   314-340-3366   (hssc.edu)
Jefferson College   636-942-3000   (jeffco.edu)
Lindenwood University   636-949-4996   (lindenwood.edu)
Logan College of Chiropractic
          636-227-2100   (logan.edu)
Malachi Bible College of St. Louis
          314-868-2979 (malachibiblecollege.edu)
Maryville University   314-529-9350   (maryville.edu)
McKendree College   314-436-3301   (mckendree.edu)
Missouri Baptist University
          314-434-1115   (mobap.edu)
St. Charles Community College
          636-922-8000   (stchas.edu)
St. Louis Christian College
          314-837-6777   (slcc4ministry.edu)
St. Louis College of Pharmacy
          314-367-8700   (stlcop.edu)
St. Louis Community College
          314-539-5000   (stlcc.edu)
Florissant Valley Campus
          314-595-4200   (stlcc.edu)
Forest Park Campus   314-644-9100   (stlcc.edu)
Meramec Campus   314-984-7500   (stlcc.edu)
St. Louis University   314-977-2222   (slu.edu)
St. Louis Parks College   618-337-9540   (slu.edu)
Southern Illinois University
          888-327-5219   (siue.edu)
University Of Missouri St. Louis
          314-516-5000   (umsl.edu)
Washington University   314-935-5000   (wustl.edu)
Webster University   314-968-6991   (webster.edu)

Going to college offers a lot of opportunities once you have a general idea of what you want to major in. Whether it is a business, music, liberal arts, journalism, broadcast or science degree, once you set in motion plans on attending a college sometimes things fall in to place better than you expected. If you're not sure about college I recommend starting at a local Junior College, where after 2 years you can graduate with an Associate of Arts degree. After 2 years in a Junior College, you will hopefully have an idea of a major field to pursue at a four-year institution. College can offer you knowledge about specific subjects for you to build your career on and it broadens your horizon in meeting people from all walks of life. To be successful in any career, a key factor is being able to communicate and interact with a lot of different people. College is one way of meeting new friends and socializing on a totally different level than what you experienced in High School.

At some schools you can apply for scholarships, grants and financial aid. Get your parents involved and fill out a FAFSA form. This is a Free Application For Federal Student Aid; most High School Counselor offices should have the form. I recommend the college issue of U.S. News & World Report, which ranks schools but also list those that are most generous in scholarships to the deserving. The only way to ensure you won't succeed in receiving scholarship money is if you don't even try to apply. I might also recommend you apply to Ivy League and private schools, which sometimes offer various packages of grants, scholarships and work programs that include paying for room, board and tuition.

Financial Aid programs to look at for college education include:

Pell Grants. Mostly given to low-income families. Money grants range from $300 to $3,000. For more information call 800-433-3243.
College Grants. Many institutions offer several types of grants, which may or not be based on financial needs. Some scholarships are awarded for high SAT/ACT scores, musicians, and athletes, among other talented skills. Check with your college of choice.

Words of Wisdom: Your right decisions determine your destiny!

Supplemental Education Opportunity Grants (SEOGs). These grants are funded by the federal government and are offered through college financial aid offices. Usually they run from $100 to $4,000. Find out by talking to the admissions office of the college you are applying to.

Resident State Programs. Many states offer grants based on a combination of merit, grades, and financial needs. Ask your High School guidance counselor for details of grants available in your state. You also might check in with Missouri Department of Higher Education-800-473-6757 or the Illinois Student Assistance Commission - 800-899-4722.

Other good places to research scholarships include: (fastweb.com), (finaid.org), (collegenet.com) and (fastaid.com). Another very good resource is a booklet published by the American Legion, "Need a Lift?" It contains 162 pages listing scholarships, loans, grants and financial aid. It can be purchased for $3.95 and ordered by calling toll-free: 1-888-453-4466.

Don't overlook Trade or Technical Schools

The following Trade Schools, Technical Colleges or Institutes offer specialized programs committed to providing a comprehensive education. They give you the training, usually in 12-24-36 months to prepare for employment in a variety of business, medical, industrial, technical, trade and secretarial fields. The costs can be less then a 4-5 year undergraduate college education and you finish in less time. Contact a particular school by asking for the admission department and have them mail you a packet of information; including class programs, degrees, scholarships and grants that are available. You can also apply for financial aid depending upon your individual situation and what income bracket your parent's fall into.

Schools of Business and Secretarial

Allied Medical College	314-739-4450	(alliedcollege.edu)
Carlson Travel Academy	314-523-5280	(carlsontravelacademy.com)
Daruby School	314-454-6933	(darubyschool.edu)
H&R Block School	314-830-9200	(hrblock.com)
Hickey College	314-434-2212	(hickeycollege.edu)
Keller Graduate School Management		
	314-542-4004	(kellergraduage.edu)

Midwest Institute	314-965-8363	(midwestinstitute.com)
Missouri College	314-821-7700	(missouricollege.com)
Missouri Tech	314-569-3600	(motech.edu)
Patricia Stevens College	314-421-0949	(patriciastevenscollege.edu)
Petropolis Academy of Pet Grooming	636-537-2322	(petropolis.com)
St. Louis College of Health Careers	314-652-0300	(slchc.com)
Sanford-Brown College	636-349-0988	(sanford-brown.net)

Career options to look at include:

-Computer Applications
-Paralegal
-Fashion Merchandising
-Business Administration
-Graphic Design
-Management Support
-Skilled Pet Groomer
-Interior Design

-Administrative Assistant
-Massage Therapy
-Accounting
-Retail Management
-Travel & Tourism
-Hospitality
-Legal Administrative Assistant
-Newly Created Position

Schools of Industrial, Trade and Technical

Acdelco Training Center	314-416-1946	(acdelco.com)
Allied College	314-739-4450	(alliedcollege.edu)
The Bartending Institute	314-997-7797	(pbsa.com)
C-1 Truck Driving Training	314-382-0002	(C1training.com)
Clayton Pet Spa	314-725-1800	(no web site)
Elaine Steven Beauty College Inc.	314-868-8196	(elainestevenbeautycollege.edu)
Goldenlands Tattoos & Accessories	314-423-0530	(goldenlands.com)
High Tech Institute	314-595-3400	(alliedcollege.edu)
L'ecole Culinaire School	314-587-2433	(lecoleculinaire.com)
Lincoln Technical Institute	877-535-4491	(lincolntech.com)

MTC Truck Driver Training
314-895-4111   (mtctruckdrivertraining.com)
Missouri College   314-821-7700   (my.missouricollege.com)
Missouri School of Barbering and Hairstyling
314-839-0310   (no web site)
Missouri School of Dog Grooming
314-428-1700   (msdg.org)
Missouri Tech College   314-569-3600   (motech.edu)
Petropolis Academy of Pet Grooming And Training
636-537-2322   (petropolis.com)
Ranken Technical Institute
314-371-0236   (ranken.edu)
St. Charles School of Massage Therapy
636-498-0777   (spastcharles.com)
St. Louis County Police Academy
314-889-8600 (stlouisco.com/police/academy)
St. Louis County Fire Academy
314-889-8670   (stlouisco.com/fire/academy)
St. Louis Job Corps Center
314-382-3948   (stljobcorp.com)
Sanford-Brown College
636-349-0988   (sanford-brown.net)
Tech Skills   314-878-1422   (techskills.com)
Tom Rose School of Pet Grooming
636-376-4273   (tomrose.com)
Vatterott College   314-890-8484   (vatterott-college.edu)

Career options to look at include:

- Office Technology
- Bartender
- Software Engineering
- Electronics Engineering
- Massage Therapist
- Multimedia
- Automotive Maintenance
- Professional Sales
- Industrial Technology
- HVAC Technology
- Cooking Chef
- Network Specialist
- Truckdriver
- Hairstylist
- Computer Drafting/Design
- Web Programming
- Bible Ministry
- Software Applications
- Computer Administrative
- Pet Groomer
- Refrigeration Technology
- Electronics Technology

-Police Officer

-Aviation Training

-Tatoo Artist

-Fire Fighter

-Computer Support Specialist

-Web Site Designer

Schools of Medical/Dental Assistants and Technicians

Allied College	314-739-4450	(hightechinstitute.edu)
Allied Medical College	314-739-1756	(hightechinstitute.edu)
Midwest Institute	314-965-8363	(midwestinstitute.com)
Missouri College	314-821-7700	(missouricollege.com)
St. Louis College of Health Careers		
	314-652-0300	(slchc.com)
Sanford-Brown College	888-224-5777	(sanford-brown.net)

Career options to look at include:

-Medical/Billing/Coding

-Medical Assistant

-Veterinary Assistant

-Medical Office Coordinator

-Respiratory Therapist

-Health Information Specialist

-Dental Assistant

-Pharmacy Technician

-Health Administration

-Medical Specialist

-Practical Nursing

-Radiography

A Look at Joining the Armed Forces

The Armed Forces have some great programs to look at. As a soldier serving in one of the branches of the Armed Forces you can serve your country as patriots before you have done. The U.S. Armed Forces offers you training in field exercises, classrooms, and working on the latest equipment with the most current technology available. They also offer you an education with college funding and the opportunity to travel and see the world, along with a great retirement program.

For example, when joining the U.S. Army they can offer you:

- Up to 100% tuition assistance.
- Up to $20,000 enlistment bonus.
- Up to $70,000 for college.
- 30 days of paid vacation a year.
- The choice of over 150 careers.
- Medical and dental care.
- Low-cost convenient shopping at the post exchange (PX) and commissary.

- Room and board.
- Professional quality sports and recreational facilities.
- Low-cost life insurance providing up to $250,000 of coverage.

Sources for Local Recruiting Programs

Air Force Recruiting	800-423-USAF	(airforce.com)
Army Recruiting	877-562-0028	(goarmy.com)
Marines Recruiting	800-MARINES	(marines.com)
Navy Recruiting	800-USA-NAVY	(navy.com)
U.S. Coast Guard	877-NOW-USCG	(gocoastguard.com)

Career options to look at include:

- Commissioned Officer
- Military Police
- Veterinary Doctor
- Flight Instructor
- Pharmacists
- Aviation Specialist
- Crane Operator
- Avionic Mechanic
- Network Systems Operator
- Cryptologic Linguists
- Military Journalist
- Military Lawyer
- Military Chaplain
- Nurse
- Jet Pilot
- Military Physician
- Electrician
- Finance Specialist
- Radio Operator
- Military Musician
- Translator/Interpreters
- Port Security Specialist

By joining the armed services you may qualify for a $65,000 grant upon completing your service obligation that can apply toward your college funding. Upon graduating bootcamp you get a smart transcript with accredited hours for classes you take in the armed forces. There are over 1250 colleges and schools that accept these credit hours. You have tuition assistance programs that can pay 100% of tuition while on active duty.

Keep in mind you can make a career of the service area you choose, by completing 19 years and 6 months. You retire with a monthly pension, full medical/dental benefits for your family (up to college age children), and you qualify for VA benefits for home and business loans. You could step out and secure a federal job with the government (Post Office/State Police/IRS) where the government buys out your military time, you still are drawing a monthly pension salary. Spend another ten years in that position and retire with full 30-year benefits from that position.

The following are some of the programs offered by the Armed Forces:

ROTC Programs – The ROTC program is offered at nearly 1,000 colleges and universities. It enables you to get an education that is paid for by the government if you qualify for this scholarship program. Once you graduate from that college you go to a branch of the service (Army, Air Force, Navy or Marines) and serve 6 years in the service. You start out as an officer with pay, having secured a 4-year college degree. This program offers the simultaneous membership, meaning that since you are "dual enrolled" in the service and the ROTC program, you will not be deployed overseas to serve.

Montgomery GI Bill (MGIB) – This is an educational assistance program enacted by Congress. Once you have completed 2 to 6 years in a specific branch of the armed services and upon completion of your service commitment, with benefits payable for ten years following your release from active duty, you are entitled to up to $35,000 to use for college education.

Tuition Assistance Programs – You can also get tuition assistance of $4,500 for each year you are enlisted in the service. It will pay up to a Masters Degree. You can select a traditional college, work with an on-line college or attend classes at the duty station of the base where you are assigned.

Loan Repayment Program – This program is for individuals who go straight to college and have graduated with an undergraduate or masters degree. Then, if you decide to join the service, you can qualify for up to $65,000 of loan repayment for your student loans.

Careers In Construction

A career in the construction industry is also another good option. Especially if you like working in different locations, you like working with your hands and physical body and you enjoy working in an outside or inside environment. Demand for workers in the construction industry is growing and will continue to increase because of the shortage of qualified construction laborers. Opportunities are expanding rapidly in the construction area and there are a wide variety of career choices.

You earn income immediately because the construction industry pays wages while you learn the craft. Apprentices starting pay ranges from $9 to $12 per hour and as you advance the wages can exceed $19 per hour. Journey-level workers are paid from $20 per hour to more than $27 per hour plus benefits. You can earn up to 45 credit hours, which is 2/3 of an associate's college degree, and the union pays for you to go to school.

My research confirms that the health benefits are awesome. Nowhere did I find a company that offers the health welfare package that the construction industry offers. They pay for you, and your family is also covered. In the corporate field, a company, after the 90-120 day waiting period, will pay a large percentage of your health insurance but you typically pay for your wife and children.

Once you are fully vested, having 5 years experience and 1200 hours during each additional year, you can retire at age 55 with a full benefits package that would pay you at today's ratio of $3500 to $4000 per month retirement income.

Here are 20 Career paths in the St. Louis Construction industry to look at:

Boilermaker – They receive four years of training in how to assemble and repair boilers, pressure vessels, tanks and vats. Contact David Snead @ 314-421-3151.

Bricklayer – Apprentices receive classroom and shop training in 8-hour sessions twice a month, learning specific aspects of bricklaying, such as constructing a block wall. Contact Tim Corcoran @ 314-770-1066.

Carpenter – They receive complete interior and exterior finish training, also build and remodel homes, commercial buildings, manufacturing plants and roadways. Carpenters can also specialize in installing concrete forms, driving pile or working as millrights. Contact Tony Caputa or Craig Hood @ 314-457-8300.

Cement Mason – They perform all types of concrete work at some of St. Louis' best known landmarks, such as sports facilities. Contact Tom Ostermeyer @314-644-1550.

Construction Craft Laborer – These apprentices receive 4,000 hours of on-the-job training and with up to 424 hours of off-site training. Laborers provide a wide variety of tasks in all areas of construction, including commercial and residential building construction, heavy and highway construction, and environmental remediation. Contact Donald Griesenauer Jr. @ 636-585-1500.

Electrician – They receive 8,000 hours of training, including instruction in data, telecommunications, instrumentation and process control wiring to match the growing needs of the information age. Contact Dennis Gralike @ 314-644-3587.

Elevator Constructor – Apprentices take classes that cover rigging, electrical construction, hydraulics and material handling. Contact George Lades @314-644-3933.

Floorlayer – A four-year training program gives floorlayer apprentices the experience they need to install all types of flooring. Contact Steve Fuller @ 314-457-8301.

Glazier – Glaziers cut, fabricate and install glass and metal glass-holding window products, including aluminum doors, storefronts, curtainwalls and skylights. Contact Dennis Stegman @ 314-644-3922.

Insulator & Asbestos Worker – These workers optimize the environment of a building by insulating mechanical systems, hot and cold piping, ducts and boilers. Contact Jim Hederman @ 314/291-1023 or call Asbestos Workers Local No. 1 @ 314-291-6993.

IronWorker – The pinnacle of an ironworker's job is topping out a construction project with the last structural beam. Ironworker's set and bolt steel beams to form the structural framework of many high-rise buildings. Contact Joe Hunt @ 314-644-1550.

Operating Engineer – They are at the helm of construction's muscle machines, including backhoe, dozers, scrapers, highlifts and cranes. Contact Ronnie Duncan @ 573-485-2200.

Painter, Wallper Hanger & Drywall Taper – Painters achieve superior skills with three years of training in painting, drywall taping, wallpapering, sandblasting, safety and decorating. Contact Timothy Klotz @ 314-647-5088.

Pipefitter – They use computers to lay out intricate designs for piping to safely deliver product to all types of industries and businesses. Contact Mark Collom @ 314-388-0722.

Plasterer – They perform all aspects of plastering, including hawk and trowel work. Contact John Davis @ 314-894-2345.

Plumber – Fountains, swimming pools, water theme parks are dependent on plumbers installing complex water supply lines and drainage systems. Contact Donald Summers Jr. @ 314-388-0722.

Roofer – Working on top of St. Louis, roofers install and repair a variety of roofing systems. They also perform waterproofing on roofs, plaza decks and parking garage floors. Contact Dan Knight @ 314-535-9683.

Sheet Metal Worker – A building's environmental system begins with sheet metal workers cutting, fabricating and installing sheet metal products for heating, ventilation and air conditioning. Sheet metal workers start as apprentices for six months, followed by 9,000 hours of on-the-job and classroom training. Contact Dan Andrews @ 314-534-9680.

Teamster – Teamsters keep projects moving by driving a variety of vehicles, including concrete mixers and material delivery trucks. They also haul debris away from construction sites. Contact Richard Mark @ 314-647-8350.

Tile Setter – In addition to on-the-job training, tile setter apprentices receive three to four years of classroom instruction. Courses cover product knowledge, math, layout, installation of products, safety procedures and blueprint reading. Contact Michael Burns @ 314-522-3779.

Source: Pride of St. Louis, Inc., 34 N. Brentwood Blvd., Suite 208, St. Louis, MO 63105 St. Louis Union Construction Industry

Be An Entrepreneur

My last area of advice is if you are not sure what you want to do... and college, learning a trade, joining the armed forces, construction or job careering does not fit your profile, then give thought to starting your own business. This can be the other side of the dial for you. But it takes careful planning and steady plotting to make this happen. Once you have your business idea in place you will want to secure money to start a company. I suggest these guidelines:

• Develop a business plan in writing
• Decide if you will have a partner or business backer
• Contact a bank or financial institution to secure funding

I found that **SCORE** (Service Corps of Retired Executives), which acts independently from the SBA, is a key resource to contact here in St. Louis. SCORE will help identify and help prepare you for starting your own business. They have a workbook-planning guide loaded with questions that will identify your potential as a business owner. The following sections apply:

Section 1 Your Business Idea

- You will need to briefly describe the product or service you plan to provide.
- What is unique about your product or service?
- Does your product or service have competition?
- How is your idea for a business different from your competitors?
- What customer need or desire does your product or service satisfy?
- List areas why you think there is sufficient customer base for your product.

Section 2 Your Self Assessment

Are you willing to risk your personal finances?
- Do you have the self-discipline to stay on course?
- Do you get along well with others?
- Do you have sales, marketing or bookkeeping skills?
- Do you have any management experience?
- Do you have the necessary financial resources?

Section 3 Operational Considerations

- This part deals with the when and how are you going to run your business.
- What exactly is the **focus** of your product or service?
- What image do you want your customer to have about your business?
- List the name of your selected business and file the necessary forms required with the government.
- Does the name of your business contribute to the image of your business?
- What type of legal structure are you going to use for your business?
- Where will your business be located?
- Is the location of your business convenient to your customer?
- What will your business hours be, and will you be open on the weekends?

Section 4 Marketing Perspectives

- Marketing is one of the most important aspects of any business.
- How well do you know your industry?

- Have you investigated the trade associations involved with your industry?
- Have you done any research in knowing your competition?
- Can you identify who is your customer?
- How do you intend to price your product or service?
- What are the key features and benefits of your product or service?
- How do the benefits of your product or service benefit the customer's needs or desires?
- What promotional method, TV, radio, print, will best suit your customer?

Section 5 Financial Assumptions

- When starting a business of your own, one of the most important steps is determining how much funding will be required to get the business up and running and self-sufficient.
- SCORE will have you work up a sales and revenue forecast.
- You will make a list of start up cost involved to set up your business.
- Do you plan to borrow money to start your business? If yes, how much?
- Do you have other owners who plan to invest in the business?
- Will there be any silent partners investing in the business?
- SCORE will help you determine the cost of producing the product or service.
- You will have to list inventory, supplies, consumables, subcontractor expenses, transportation cost, among other areas.
- SCORE will help you identify operating expenses.
- SCORE will help you determine additional assets required after start up for your business, such as equipment, computers, furniture, fixtures, automobiles, etc.

SCORE Contact information: Phone: 314-539-6600 x242 (ask for a counselor) Web site: (info@stlscore.org)

SBA Financial Assistance

The SBA (Small Business Administration) is Congressionally mandated to assist the nation's small businesses in meeting their financing needs. The agency's finance programs enhance the ability of lenders to provide short-term and long-term loans to small businesses that might not qualify through normal lending channels.

Basic 7(a) Loan Guaranty Program – This is the SBA's primary loan program. It is also the most flexible, since the agency can guarantee financing under the program for a variety of general business purposes. To qualify for an SBA guaranty, a small business must meet the 7(a) loan guaranty criteria, and the lender must certify that it cannot provide funding on reasonable terms except with an SBA guaranty. The SBA can guarantee up to 85% of a loan that is $150,000 or less and 75% on loans greater than $150,000. The maximum size loan that the SBA can guarantee is $2 million, and the maximum guaranty that the SBA can provide is $1 million. For information on this loan visit (sba.gov/financing/fr7aloan.html.)

For more information locally contact: e-Center for Business, U.S. Small Business Administration, 200 North Broadway, Suite 1500, St. Louis, MO 63102. Phone: 314-539-6600. Web site: (sba.gov)

You may also contact your local bank or other lending institutions, but you will need to have a written business plan. Contact SCORE to help you achieve this written business plan, which should include a cover letter, Executive Summary, Operational Section, Marketing Section, and Financial Section.

I suggest you might also contact the **BBB** (Better Business Bureau) to see if any businesses like the one you are starting have any major complaints.

Contact information: BBB, 12 Sunnen Drive, Suite 121, St. Louis, MO 63143. Phone: 314-645-0606 Web site: (contactbbb.org)

Other online resources to learn more about small-business programs:

Small Business Training Network, the SBA's virtual campus with free training courses, workshops, and more to assist entrepreneurs, (sba.gov/training)

Online Women's Business Center that promotes the growth of women-owned businesses, (onlinewbc.gov)

Department of Labor, which deals with compliance assistance, (dol.gov/osbp/sbrefa/main.htm)

Minority Business Development, which fosters the establishment and growth of minority-owned businesses, (mbda.gov)

Business government, which is the link to the U.S. government that has information about business development, financial assistance, taxes, laws and regulations and workplace issues, (business.gov)

> *Words of Wisdom for starting a business: Find a need... and fill it!*

Be a Volunteer and Join the Peace Corps

For those of you looking to do something different for a while, you might think about joining the Peace Corps. If you have a commitment to do service in helping others in a foreign country, a desire to travel, a good work ethic, and generous spirit of giving, this might make a great learning adventure and a dream come true. You will learn to speak the local language, work in villages, cities and towns around the world. Volunteers participate in the culture and the values of the people they serve. Volunteers who join the Peace Corps must be at least 18 years of age, have good health, and be a U.S. citizen. You will need to have a variety of work experience and education levels among other skills to accept the challenge. To get a full understanding of the Peace Corps see below.

Contact information:
Peace Corps Recruitment Office for Missouri is Chicago Region, 55 West Monroe Street, Suite 450, Chicago, IL 60603
Phone: 312-353-4990   Web site: (chicago@peacecorps.gov)
Phone: 800-424-8580   Web site: (peacecorps.gov)

Contact information:
Americorps, which is a similar program to the Peace Corps.
Phone: 800-942-2677   Web site: (americorps.org)

GOAL SETTING

Finding Your Direction in Life

What is success to you? Work to develop a philosophy of success that fits your personality. Life is a series of events that will go on for the next 50-75 years. All aspects of life-personal, friendship, business, marriage and family, are interrelated as you grow in maturity. Your physical, mental and spiritual lives are connected and all these areas will impact the financial aspects of your life.

Goal setting is an important area to develop in your daily routine on life's pathway to older age. By setting goals you can reach out to finish points you create and find accomplishments you might have thought you could have never achieved. This chapter will discuss how goal setting can be **KEY** to the planning stages for many years to come. What are some goals you want out of life? In my 50 years of living, I have identified 10 goals that I want out of life. They are the following:

John Eyres 10 Point "I want out of Life" Goal List

1. To be happy.
2. To be healthy and exercise regularly.
3. To watch the foods I eat, especially sweets.
4. To have good family relationships.
5. To attend Church on a regular basis.
6. To be financially successful within reason.
7. To be secure.

8. To have peace of mind.
9. To always enjoy my job.
10. To have hope, faith and love be a mainstay in my life.

Now write down your own 10 point philosophy list of what you want out of life:

1. _____
2. _____
3. _____
4. _____
5. _____
6. _____
7. _____
8. _____
9. _____
10. _____

Creating Goals and Writing Them Down

Having goals in life and writing them down on paper and viewing them on a daily basis is a key objective for your continued success. You need to develop short-term, intermediate, and long-term goals. You must have a planned direction utilizing your ability, education, training and life's philosophy to the fullest. A goal list becomes like a blueprint to building a house or directions to putting a bicycle together. Think about it! You wouldn't plan a trip to Florida to see the ocean without a plan would you? You would need a road map to get there, lodging at a motel when you arrive, various sights to see along the way, saved up money, etc...

Years ago I attended two night classes at Dale Carnegie Institute and I remember one of the instructors saying that people with a "goals program" can earn more than twice as much money as those without goals. They are also happier and healthier and get along better with people they work and live with. These people tend to have more friends, more peace of mind, more security and more hope for the future. Those two classes taught me a lot about people, communications and setting goals, and why these qualities contribute to a longer and more rewarding life. I personally have never met a depressed person who had specific long-range goals and a plan of action to reach them.

Power of Goal Setting

The power of goal setting is that by laying down a written goal, making it happen, expecting a desired result and then achieving that goal takes **EFFORT** on your part. It's huge...and then you reach that goal. Accomplishment, satisfaction, pay-off, excitement are just a few words to describe what you set forth to do and then **DID IT**! But until you list your goals and have a written plan attached to them you are not a goal setter or goal achiever.

GOAL + WRITTEN PLAN + ACTION + EXPECTATION + CONFESSION = ACHIEVEMENT!

Be a Dreamer

The first step to reaching dreams is to have them. Start asking yourself what you want in life. These goals must be realistic and attainable within reason. Don't be afraid to think outside of the box for your goals. Think about great men of history who dared to dream; Columbus set forth sailing across the seas to the New World, hoping the world was not flat. Lewis & Clark were great explorers and dreamers and adventurers, they carved out a map taking them from Ohio all the way to the far Northwest coast of America. Another man who dared to dream and speak out loud about it was Muhammad Ali, the greatest boxer of all time. He said, "I am the greatest boxer of all time, I move like a butterfly and sting like a bee, no man is greater than me!" I challenge you to go to the library and check out a book about a great man or woman in history that you can identify with and study their success patterns and I'm sure somewhere you will find they set goals to get where they wanted!

Talk to people about their goals and dreams and how they have achieved them. What was their strategy? How did they create an action plan? Begin right now to develop your own style, personalized need to meet your desires and cravings in life!

Setting Goals Will Establish Your Direction

Take "quiet time" so you can think about what goals you want. Again I suggest a place outdoors, I find nature more conducive to helping me to relax and open my mind clearer. Write them down on paper and put notes next to each goal as to questions/answers, as to how to achieve that specific task. Create deadlines for your goals; give definite dates so you have a time line and framework needed to complete each given goal. Deadlines have a way of motivating us to produce **RE-SULTS**. The activities you plot on paper can have shorter time periods within each long-term goal. For example – part of my goal is to lose 10 pounds in the next 3 months, and lose another 10 pounds in the next 3 months, and then lose 5 pounds over the next 3 month period, ending with 5 more pounds the last 3 months of the year. At the end of the year I will have lost 30 pounds. This divide and conquer approach keeps your goals from becoming too overwhelming.

After writing down your goals, make sure you view them daily and speak them out loud. This reinforces the goal in your subconscious mind. I put my goals and faith statements on my bathroom mirror and look at them every morning and say them aloud. By making declarations daily, controlling what comes out of your mouth, saying positive vs. the negative will definitely have an impact. When I was eight or nine years old my mom sat me down on the couch one evening after my homework and shared her words of wisdom to me. One golden nugget of wisdom kept with me the rest of my life. She told me the word "hate" had very negative vibrations and that I should never use the word "hate" ever. Growing up in grade school I learned to erase that word from my vocabulary and it did have an impact on my life. The other gem she asked me to do was every day at school give three people a nice compliment. I like your hair. I like that shirt you're wearing. Congratulations on scoring a 100 on your math test. I grew up giving three daily positives to people and I have carried that on into my adulthood. Speaking out positive statements does have an impact on you, the people around you and the way you live your life.

Make your goals realistic and running parallel with your life. Have short-term goals (less then a year), intermediate goals (3-5 years) and long-term goals (10-20 years). If your goal is to be a millionaire, realize it will not happen overnight and you will need to have a stronger, very finely tuned series of goals to probably achieve that milestone. And if you are in a job now making $25,000, you must realize the millionaire goal is not out of reach, it's just entails reaching longer, harder and more sacrifice on your part.

One of my goals, which I had decided in Junior High, was to travel to Europe and see all the ancient ruins, castles, and art museums, travel the countryside and meet many people of different cultures. My mom was instrumental in having me start a list of goals on a 4 X 6 index card and tape that to my bedroom mirror. Every morning and every night when I went to bed I would look at those goals, the number one goal on the top of the list was my trip to Europe. I thought about it and dreamed about it and always had my goal growing up that I would go to that far away land across the Atlantic Ocean. When I graduated college in 1977 I started looking at how I would achieve the goal. I found out about a program for students and teachers based out of the University of Illinois that offered an 8-week 18-country tour of Europe. I paid the money, which was less then $2000.00 at that time, and went on the trip of my lifetime in the summer of 1978. Wow, at age 23 I successfully completed a goal I had set 11 years earlier. It was a wonderful feeling knowing all those years that I would travel to Europe someday and finally that "someday" arrived. It was a great sense of accomplishment for me.

Keep on Setting Goals all Your Life

Develop a sincere desire for the goals you really want. Cut out pictures from a magazine; take photographs of your goal. If it is a new car as your goal, go to the car dealership and drive that car, smell the leather, feel the smooth ride, experience the thrill of driving that car. Ask for a brochure on that car, take it home and tape it up on your bathroom or bedroom mirror to look at **EVERY** day. Pictures can paint words that we don't know how to describe. The important thing to do is keep setting your goals, even if they start out small, but continue making them all your life. Goals will move you in the direction you want to be heading. So never give up and never stop making goals, they will help you more than hurt you.

I recommend you keep your goals to yourself. Don't tell very many people what your personal goals are. Telling others may breed negative energy and doubt. Their unbelief in what you have planned can cast a shadow of defeat on your inner self-abilities. Tell your dreams and goals only to people who support you and believe in your capabilities to get to the finish line.

Review your goals and as you progress you might need to make adjustments and changes. That's **OK**! Because at least you are heading in a direction mode and eventually you **WILL** get there **IF** you don't give up, cave in, or quit. Have persistence, which I think is a critical key to succeeding in your goals. It doesn't matter how much education you have, how genius you are, if your parents have no money, nothing works better/stronger/faster for you then persistence and determination in getting your goals accomplished.

Start Your Own Personal "Goal Notebook"

Please take the time to buy a notebook, find that quiet place again and begin your own personal "Goal Notebook." I suggest a setting outside with nature, this always helps me to relax and fine-tune my inner man, spirit, soul and body. Choose a setting by a park, by a lake, by a spacious field with trees and sit quietly and reflect upon your inner-self to fill in the blanks to my 10 point goal charting for your life over the next 35+ years.

1.   **Career/Profession**-How can you improve yourself at your job? How can you find more happiness and peace at work? What can you do to strengthen your relationship with your co-workers or supervisor?
2.   **Health/Physical Body**-What are your goals concerning exercise? What are you doing to take care of your body so you can age slowly and wonderfully? What do you want to weigh at the end of the year? What foods or drinks do you need to stay away from?
3.   **Personal Appearance**-What changes do you want to make to your wardrobe, make-up, hairstyle, your personal style concerning your appearance?
4.   **Financial**-How much money will you make this year? How much money do you want to be making in 5 years? In 10 Years? In 20 years? How much money will you save in a year?
5.   **Self-Development**-What books, fiction and non-fiction, do you plan to read this year? What about listening to certain set of motivational tapes? What about attending special events, lectures or grand openings to broaden your horizons?
6.   **Creativity**-How can you use your creativity to improve your way of life? What changes can you make to your apartment or home to make things different? How much time each day can you set aside for creative think-tank time?
7.   **Family**-How can you be a better family member? How can you

improve your relationships with your parents, siblings, spouse, or children?

8. **Personal Relationships**–What can you do to effectively increase relationships with your friends, spouse, co-workers, boss and neighbors?

9. **Special Interest**–What hobbies, special focus can you spend in your free time? What new sports can you try? What softball, volleyball, or bowling team can you sign up to play on? Do you want to try gardening or mountain climbing? Where do you want to go on vacation?

10. **Fun**–What is it you can do on special weeknights or one weekend a month to just have **FUN**, let loose, be yourself and enjoy yourself? Is it a weekend camp trip or ice skating one evening at Forest Park? Is it an occasional music concert at UMB Bank Pavillion?

Reward Yourself For Accomplishing A Goal

You need to give yourself a reward of some kind when you accomplish a major goal. Whether you go out to dinner with a friend to celebrate, go shopping to buy some new clothes, or just go buy a dozen Krispy Kreme donuts...**CELEBRATE**! Make sure to treat yourself with some pleasure/enjoyment/happiness for accomplishing your goal. Maybe take a day off work and take a 3-day weekend trip to see a friend in another town. If you like to play golf take an afternoon off from work and go play 9 holes with a close friend. If your budget is tight plan accordingly, treat yourself to a movie. Buy the large popcorn and soda combo and smile real big as you munch and slurp to your hearts content. Creating workable goals for yourself and keeping disciplined to follow your plan deserves a reward. It makes goal-setting a stronger part of your life. Your attitude determines your altitude (how high you fly) and your direction determines your destiny.

Follow my M.A.R.C.S. Target Plan Toward Your Goals

Measurable–Plan to measure your goals week-by-week, month-by-month and year-by-year. You can't measure exactly if your happiness has improved but if you feel better and smile more often you have achieved some progress in reaching your goals. For example if you want to lose weight, part of your goal program might be to exercise at the YMCA on Monday, Wednesday and Friday mornings before work. At the end of the week give yourself a review test to see if you accomplished each step. If you measure your mini goals week by week then measurable progress toward your larger goal of losing 20 pounds by the end of the year becomes a stronger reality.

Attainable–Many people set goals that are not attainable. Start with some small goals and achieve a little success at first. Don't set impossible goals that can't be reached. This ends in defeat and a negative poor self-esteem. The longer-term goals can have more challenges but that's okay because you have a longer time frame to accomplish them and also make adjustments along the way. Again set goals you know you can accomplish when first starting your goal making process. And remember I believe it is better to set a goal, accomplish most or all of it then **never** set any goals at all.

Realistic–Be open and honest with yourself. Set realistic goals that with hard work and perseverance can be achieved. Take the amount of time needed to carefully plan and map out your goals. By being true to yourself, believing in your heart that you can accomplish the target marks you aiming for, and then you will hit the bulls eye with accuracy you desire.

Character–Build up your inner-self person to rise above all the adversities that will face you along the way. Develop that "never give up, cave-in or quit" attitude and you will find that your dreams and desires can come true, it can happen to you. Never waiver from the qualities that make you the individual you are and strive for moral excellence to uphold your integrity to the mission at hand. Look at yourself daily in the mirror and say, "Every day in every way I **AM** getting better and better and I am sewing good seeds to my own *success*!"

Specific–Be specific in setting up your goals. Clearly identify your target with adjectives that spell out deeper meaning for your goals. Not just "I'm going to own a new car." Be more detailed and phrase the goal with, "I'm going to own a red, 1964 convertible Chevy Corvette with chrome wheels and black leather interior." Make each goal special and give it details that get you excited when you read it aloud each day.

How do You Take Your Medicine?

Mouth   = Speaking out loud your goals!
Ears   = Hearing and listening to tapes by successful people to help achieve your goals!
Eyes   = Dreaming and visualizing with your "Third Eye" to see your goals!

Speaking Out Words Can Make a Huge Impact in Your Life

The power of the tongue is key to affecting your attitude. Making positive affirmations out loud on a daily basis is a proven technique used by many motivational speakers. Every day I encourage you to go over the following statements, saying them aloud to yourself in front of a mirror:

"I am making the right decisions in my life!"
"I am happy, healthy and wise and heading in a positive life direction."
"I have vision in my life and I see things not only with my eyes but also with my heart."
"People like me and I have favor with everyone I come in contact with."
"I am a Winner I am NOT a loser!"
"To achieve something I really desire or want, I am going to have to do something I've never done."
"What ever I can conceive, I can believe and achieve it!"

Add a couple more "Positive Phrases" to make your own personal affirmation statements!

NOTES:

3

SETTING UP A BUDGET

Budget Now, Borrow Less Later

Why set up a budget in the first place? As you get a job down the road of life you will have "money coming in" from your job and "money going out" paying your bills and expenses. The purpose of a budget is to guide you, not confine you. A budget is basically very simple, you have a given amount of money to spend. A budget helps you decide how you're going to spend that money for the coming year. It also helps you live within your means and **NOT** go into debt. One of the most important keys to having a budget and working to stay on that spending guide is that you don't break the system and go into debt. Please...please...work very hard to keep out of debt. Going into debt **WILL** cost you down the road for many years to come.

By living on a budget you can calculate how much you have to spend a month in each category, such as food, housing, gasoline and entertainment. A budget also tells you how much to save each month for quarterly expenses such as car insurance, life insurance, retirement, a new car, a college fund for the kids or your annual vacation. Keep in mind that the first year or two of creating and working with a budget can be challenging, but once you master living by a budget you will be rewarded in the years to come.

Starting a Budget

The first step is to determine how much money is available each month and where it is presently being spent. Get out some paper and pencils and your calculator and make this exercise something you put careful planning into. Write down how much money is "coming in" from every source. (When you are single it is a little easier to track your money, once you get married it is a good idea to sit down and begin the budget strategy process over again with your new mate). Include your yearly salary from your job, bonuses, commissions, gifts, money from any investments and even income tax refunds. That total for the year is your "money in"; then divide the total amount by 12 and this becomes your monthly budget.

"Money IN"   *Amount*

- Salary/Wages
  (Work with take home, not gross)   _____
- Salary/Wages (spouse)   _____
- Bonuses   _____
- Commissions (estimate carefully)   _____
- Tips   _____
- Child Support   _____
- Tax Refunds   _____
- Sale of Assets   _____
- Other Income   _____
-                                       _____

TOTAL   _____

The next step is to determine how much money you spend and where. The best way to help identify your spending is to look at your last 12 months of your checkbook. (In Chapter Four we will talk about setting up a checking account when you graduate High School). If you have not done this yet, my suggestion is to start a daily diary book. Write down in the diary what and where you are spending money for about 3 months and this should help you estimate your expenses better. Work to divide your expenses into categories such as housing, automobile, insurance, food, clothing, taxes, etc. This becomes your "Money OUT" chart.

"Money OUT"   *Amount*

(Debts/Fixed Accounts)

- Home Mortgage   _____
- Rent   _____
- Auto Loan(s)   _____
- Credit Card Visa   _____
- Credit Card Kohl's   _____
- Credit Card Phillips 66   _____
- Medical Bills   _____
- Installment Loans   _____
- Bank Loans   _____
- Personal Loans   _____
- Life Insurance   _____
- Auto Insurance   _____
- Medical Insurance   _____
- Electricity   _____
- Water   _____
- Gas   _____
- Sewer   _____
- Garbage   _____
- Cable TV   _____
- DSL Line   _____
- Phone/Cell phone   _____
- Child Support
- _____
- _____

(Other expenses/day to day)

- Food   _____
- Clothing   _____
- Home repairs   _____
- Auto repairs   _____
- Gas for cars (could be cash/charge)   _____
- School loans   _____
- Contributions   _____
- Subscriptions/books   _____
- Personal expenses   _____

- Private music lessons   _____
- Little league registration   _____
- Auto registration/licenses   _____
- Pet equals food/shots/upkeep   _____
- Home improvement   _____
- Furniture   _____
- Child day care   _____
- Gifts (birthdays/anniversaries)   _____
- Recreation   _____
- Emergency account   _____
- Savings   _____
-   _____
-   _____

TOTAL   _____

Keep in mind everyone will have a different "Money OUT" list. The fixed list needs to be as close to the correct dollar amount as you can get, where as the day to day expenses, known as variable, allow you more control over these expenses.

The final step is to draw up a realistic budget for the next 12 months. Plan to spend 1-2 days in creating this budget – don't be in a hurry, take your time and work together strategically if you are now married. A goal here (key point) is that the sum of all the categories in your budget should amount to less than 100% of your total income or "Money IN".

Here are some estimates for what the average family spends in each budget category:

Housing– 32% This includes house payments, taxes, repairs and utilities.

Automobile–15% This includes payments, license plates, renewals, repairs, gasoline and insurance.

Insurance–5% This includes insurance not paid by your employer, such as life insurance, health insurance add-ons. (This category can sometimes be closer to 10% with a family).

Food–15% This relates to food and other necessities such as toilet paper, soap, detergent, deodorant, etc.

Entertainment/Recreation–7% This includes dining out, attending movies, vacations, and little league. This category must be carefully controlled for your budget to work!

Clothing–5% Choose carefully the clothes you buy.

Savings–5% This can be savings for retirement, and for unanticipated expenditures such as new appliances or new carpet for the house.

Debt–5% This includes payment on credit cards and loans. (But not the house or car).

Miscellaneous–6% This category often eats up your entire surplus, all the extras that makes your money vanish quickly, includes haircuts, cosmetics, lunch money, cash spending.

Source Information: Larry Burkett, Answers to Your Family's Financial Questions

Balancing your budget will take patience, to sit down and add up all the areas. Get that calculator warmed up and refer to your budget-planning outline and follow these three steps:

1. Total all sources of "Money IN" and record the amount on the line titled Total Cash Available.
2. Total all the expenses of "Money OUT" and record the amount on the line titled Total Cash to be Spent.
3. Subtract the amount of the total cash to be Spent from the amount of the Total Cash Available. Put that number on the line titled positive or negative.

Your Budget

From January/year to January/following year

"Money IN"	*Monthly Goal*
1. _____	_____
2. _____	_____
3. _____	_____
4. _____	_____
5. _____	_____
6. _____	_____

Total Cash Available _____

"Money OUT"	Monthly Goal
1. _____	_____
2. _____	_____
3. _____	_____
4. _____	_____
5. _____	_____
6. _____	_____
7. _____	_____
8. _____	_____
9. _____	_____
10. _____	_____
11. _____	_____
12. _____	_____
13. _____	_____
14. _____	_____
15. _____	_____
16. _____	_____
17. _____	_____
18. _____	_____
19. _____	_____
20. _____	_____

TOTAL Cash to be Spent   _____
Positive (+)   _____
Negative (-)   _____

If the number is positive, you have a surplus. You spend less than you earn. That's a good thing! But before you get too excited go back and review all your expenses carefully to make sure the numbers are accurate and/or realistic. Then I suggest you add up the numbers 2-3 times on the calculator to make sure the final figures are correct.

If...your number lands in the negative, you have a deficit. Hey, that's Okay! You are spending more than your income earned. Don't be discouraged by the deficit number. A lot of people fall into this dilemma with their budget. My wife and I have been here many times over the years. We constantly have to make adjustments to our spending to keep a balanced budget working. Over the 25 years we have been married we have been in debt 3 different times and have always carefully and strategically climbed our way out by curbing our spending and making the necessary alterations that had to be made.

Balancing the Budget

Basically you have two decisions to work with. The first choice is to decrease your spending habits and the second choice is to increase your income.

Option One – Cut Back on Spending

Balancing your budget can be difficult at times because you often make spending decisions based upon want, desire, and need issues. I want a new car vs. buying a used car. I desire to live in West County vs. living in Maplewood. I need to buy new clothes every month. Stop...and draw a line in the sand and realize you might not be where you want to be money wise. Sit down and carefully go over your day-to-day expenses, review each one meticulously and ask yourself, "Can this expense be deleted, reduced or postponed?" Don't be in a hurry – budgets take time to develop and time to balance and time to come together in the right mode.

The following list is a suggested guideline to help you cut back on spending:

1. **Take your lunch to work** – Pack a lunch rather then buy lunch every day.
2. **Find a friend-do a trade** – Ask a friend to help trim your hair, or color and cut a different style. Do a trade with that person – they cut your hair you wash their car. My wife learned to cut hair growing up with 4 brothers and ever since we have been married she has cut my hair/and trimmed my beard. Example: Savings of $15.00/month times 12 months equals $180 per year, times 25 years equals $4500.
3. **Use Coupons** – Newspapers and junk mail bring you all kinds of savings every day, including coupons for restaurants, oil lube jobs, tires, brakes, clothes, etc.
4. **Study the sales** – Best time to buy clothes is at the end of the season, carpet sales usually hit on holiday weekends, as well as furniture and major appliances.
5. **Call your insurance agent** – Ask your agent about getting higher deductibles on your car and homeowners insurance, that

means lower premiums. Note: Stay with one company and bundle all your insurance for car, home, life – you can get better rates.

6. **Buy secondhand (used)** – It is always cheaper and sometimes the best way to go when you're on a tight budget. Used car, appliance, furniture, etc. can be found easy at garage sales, swap meets, and home auctions.

7. **Live in a smaller affordable starter home first** – Don't over extend yourself, buy small, fix it up and then sell for a profit and move up in housing gradually.

8. **Use cash when shopping** – When buying food, clothes, furniture take cash instead of a credit card, it helps you limit your impulse buying.

9. **Make lists** – Make lists of food you plan to cook for the week (adapt your menu to meats & special foods that are on sale that week) and buy only what you have on the list. I make lists whenever I go to shop, to Walgreens, Target or even Home Depot.

10. **Pay cash for gas** – Another way to watch your spending dollars is to pay gas with cash as much as you can. Only when you don't have the bucks and the car is on low, use the credit card.

11. **When buying with credit card, always ask the cash price** – When buying a large ticket item compare the "charge it" price with the cash price. Even though it's six months deferred payments, no interest for six months, look carefully at pricing.

12. **Get some of your videos, CD's, DVD's, and books free** – Keep in mind that by going to your local library you can have a selection of all the above with no cost, a library card is free, you merely have the investment of time to register for one.

13. **Drop your cable or dish network monthly bill and do without 60+ channels** – Compare the money you can save here; estimated $30 to $45 dollars a month, times 12 months equals $360 to $540 in savings a year.

14. **Turn the thermostat either up or down** – Save money by turning the thermostat up higher in the summer and lowering the thermostat in the winter, and wearing a sweater or flannel shirt around the house.

15. **Car pool to work with fellow employees** – It could save some mileage on your car as well as dollars in your pocket by car pooling to work.

16. **Grow a small garden in the summer** – For the cost of a couple packets of seeds, and some tomato plants, growing fresh vegetables will be healthy and cost saving.

17. **Avoid eating out** – It costs money to eat out, whether you choose fast food, or a restaurant, including soda, beer and tips really zaps your cash.

18. **Look at the option of dropping your cell phone** – I know it might not sound pretty or cool, but if you're paying $50 a month on a cell phone, that's $600 a year you can put somewhere else to pay bills.

19. **Visit resale shops to buy your clothes and household items** – You can find great bargains on clothes and simple household nick nacks and remember – you won't always be shopping at the resale store.

20. **Ask your family and friends** – Ask people how they save money. Be wise and thrifty, ask older people to share their knowledge – including mom, dad, grandma and grandpa, even Aunt Adele.

Option Two – Increase Your Income

Remember the key to your budget is that your total expenditures (Money OUT) must not exceed your income (Money IN). But in certain circumstances you will be unable to reduce expenditures enough to balance the budget. When this happens, you must look at increasing your income.

If you are by yourself and not married, sometimes adding a part-time job can meet the required income to pay all your expenditures. Look carefully at what **YOU** can do part-time, where you can make decent money 1-2 nights a week and/or maybe work on Saturdays. Can you clean houses, do yardwork, get a grass cutting job, baby-sit, house-sit for people on the weekends, pet-sit, detail cars, sew clothes? I encourage you to sit down and make a list of 15 jobs you can do to earn extra money. When you have paid off your debts, decide if you want to quit the job or keep it for extra savings money.

If one spouse is unemployed, a part-time or full time job may help to increase income. Two incomes working together can make a big difference. Be careful when adding a second income earner to the family, make sure you have money left over after paying for childcare, a second car, clothing, lunches and taxes. (You need to be clear on how much social security, state and federal taxes are taken out to make sure it benefits you). Is that second income actually cost effective?

Another way to increase your income is by lowering your taxes. Talk to your bank or a financial planner to see what tax laws can assist you with shelters and deductions. Two ways to help shelter your money are by owning a home and funding a retirement. (Both of these are covered in later chapters).

By owning a home you have to pay property taxes and interest on a mortgage. The itemized deductions will reduce your taxable income dollar for dollar if you can qualify. By funding a retirement account such as a 401 (k) at work or qualifying for an IRA you can reduce your taxable income dollar for dollar. As you grow older these are two very important investments you will want to make.

Final Key Points in Controlling Your Budget

Make budgeting a family affair. Both you and your spouse should participate and work together on the budget. Sit down each month at a designated time (usually the bulk of bills are paid around the 10th or the 15th of the month) and pay bills together. Split up the work however you see fit, one spouse writes the checks and the other one address envelopes, marking paid on the monthly budget sheet and then stuffs envelopes with the checks. This way each mate knows exactly where the money is being spent.

Don't be a control freak. Some couples watch their spending down to the very last penny. Don't go to extremes with spending because many times the husband or wife is trying to control the others spending. Live and work; spend and budget...happily together!

Balance your checkbook. You need to be committed to balancing your checkbook every month down to the last nickel. If you need help contact your bank, they have forms on how to balance a checkbook.

Be disciplined in budgeting. Some people don't maintain the discipline to stay on a budget. Before you know it, however depressing it may be, you'll find yourself climbing out of a deep financial hole. If you just think about it too long and not ever apply a budget system, financial debt can creep up from the basement rather quickly.

Watch out for the "little debt won't hurt." Be careful of impulse buying and spending. Watch out for that special 4-day vacation to Mexico that is too expensive, that car I just got to have, or the costly gift I had to spend on Grandma. Little debt grows and grows like a cancer tumor and eventually you find yourself borrowing money just to make payments on the money you borrowed. Limit debt from the start. Bite its head off as soon as it arises!

Take a money management class. When you get married (or while you're single) I recommend you and your spouse take a non-credit course at the local area college on "money management" or personal finance."

Build an "emergency savings account." When possible, as soon as you can, start setting aside extra money to fund a special money account. This if for emergencies such as "unexpected" repairs, medical expenses, appliance failures, job layoff, etc. This safety net, once you can build it up to $1000-$10,000, gives you some peace of mind knowing you have an emergency money fund. Note: Take ½ the money you get from your wedding and devote that to emergency fund, do an extra job for 6 months, put every extra dime into this account.

Get on a monthly utility budget plan. Contact your utility companies and ask them to explain their monthly budget plans. When you have lived in a residence 6-12 months they can offer you a set monthly payment and once a year they will adjust your monthly payment up or down, depending upon rate changes and your consumption level.

Stay out of debt. At all costs work to keep from going in debt. If you have to restructure debt, shop around for lower interest rates on charge accounts. You may want to consolidate your debt with a home equity line of credit. Your interest rate should be lower than rates charged by credit card companies. Plus your interest on a home equity line will be tax deductible. (I'll discuss debt more in the next chapter).

Take a vacation week once a year. I believe a week of vacation to get away from it all is vital to your peace of mind, your marriage and your inner man/woman time away from home. Decide on a trip somewhere, calculate the dollar amount and discipline yourself to put that money aside every month. You can reduce vacation costs by taking a camping vacation, or ask friends if they have a lake/river house you can rent cheap for a week. But...by all means do yourself a huge reward, go on vacation once a week every year!

Don't Forget to Set up Your Office/Work/Billing Area

One last item to put on your list when setting up your budget is to create a simple but efficient work desk area. If you have a spare room in the house or apartment, find a cheap desk at a garage sale or look at inexpensive desk modules at Office Max or Office Depot. You can pick something up for between $75 to $150. The desk can hold your computer, which as soon as you can afford a desktop/laptop is money well spent. I recommend taking the time (hours invested) and set up your office/desk area right the first time. You will have an initial investment but decide how to best organize your desk system, including file drawers, stacked bins, or cardboard boxes. I also suggest purchasing a software package like Quicken @ $60, Home Budget for Dummies @$20, or Microsoft Money @$30, (they are worth their weight in gold).

The following is a brief list to get started with your home office:

- Computer desktop and printer. (If you can afford a scanner/fax/copy machine go for it)
- File cabinets; look at two drawers or four drawers.
- Paper, paper clips, envelopes (3 ½ X 6 ½" & 4-⅛ X 9 ½"), stamps.
- Scissors, stapler, tape dispenser, rubber bands, pens & pencils, whiteout.
- An assortment of manila folders and larger size envelopes for mailing and filing.
- Quicken software (look on E-bay for an older version).
- Calendar, notebook wide ruled (10 ½ X 8"), management planner folder.
- Boxes (from your work) to store old records in garage/basement.

Recommended books include:

Budget, by Leslie E. Linfield, FLA Publishing.
The Everything Budgeting Book, by Tere Drenth, Adams Media Corporation.

NOTES:

_____

_____

_____

_____

_____

_____

_____

_____

_____

_____

_____

_____

_____

_____

_____

_____

_____

_____

_____

_____

_____

_____

_____

_____

_____

NOTES:

_____

_____

_____

_____

_____

_____

_____

_____

_____

_____

_____

_____

_____

_____

_____

_____

_____

_____

_____

_____

_____

_____

_____

_____

_____

_____

ESTABLISHING CREDIT HISTORY

Understanding Your Credit Score and What it Means

Your credit score is a key factor in determining your access to credit, and the interest rate you'll be charged. The list for credit score and how it is used continues to grow. Auto and Homeowners insurance companies are looking at credit scores to gauge customer's future claims and setting premiums accordingly. More employers are screening job applications by credit scores. Some landlords consult them before renting. By understanding how important your credit score is we can proceed with my four-step method to establishing "basic" credit history.

Getting Started

The first step to do upon graduating from High School is to open your "very own" checking account. It helps to serve two main purposes; one, it will make working your budget planning down the road easier, and two, lenders require 2 months of checking statements when you decide to purchase a home. This way they can access your spending/ budgeting habits and view how well you handle money. Shop around for the bank that fits your needs, many offer free checking accounts, online services, special rates on certificates of deposit and so forth. Consult mom and dad for their advice, opening an account at their bank might be easier and the best follow through method. Keep in mind you want to establish a long-term relationship with your bank that can reap rewards down the road, such as a car loan or home loan in the years ahead.

The second step I recommend is to open up three charge accounts, also known as trade lines in the mortgage industry. Note that the key here is establishing credit, you're **NOT** looking to jump into the land of "charge it" and build up any debt. I believe the following 3 charge card categories will help to serve this purpose:

1. **Visa, Discover or MasterCard**–A major credit card can be started usually for a minimum balance of $500, and after months of paying on time your credit limit can increase. (Contact your bank first to see what major card they offer).

2. **Target, Kohl's, Best Buy**–You will be purchasing clothes, make-up, hair products, CD's somewhere down the road, pick one card that suits your personal needs.

3. **Shell, Phillips 66 or Mobil**–A gas card will serve a purpose for purchasing gas, oil and even car repairs.

Again, realize you only select one credit card from each category. Just charge $20 to $30 each month and pay if off every month. Start out your charge spending knowing that at the end of each month you **WILL** pay off that charge – **NO** exceptions! The first month you're unable to pay your credit card (any specific one), put it away in a drawer until you get caught up. If this doesn't work, cut up the credit card immediately. If you follow this pattern you will never have any problems with credit cards.

The third step is to start establishing rental history. A lender will review your rental payments to see that you have taken responsibility to pay consistently for a roof over your head. Most lenders will require a 12-month history of rental or mortgage payments. Some lenders will want a full 2-year history. Please note – late payments that are over 30 days late become a huge problem in buying a house. Be very careful to avoid making rental/house payments over 30 days late.

Lenders will want to verify that you have paid a monthly housing expense on time for 12-24 months. To verify your payment history you'll need copies of canceled checks or money orders. Lenders will ask for written letters sometimes from apartment or management companies. If you rent from a landlord who is an individual and not a management company they will not just take their word that you have paid on time. This is where canceled checks become key evidence to suffice for the lender. They will usually ask for at least 12 months of canceled checks to prove that you pay your housing expense on time every month. (With your own checking account this is not a problem).

My advice is those living at home or with a family member should start paying them rent. Make it a significant amount, at least $100, paying by check or money order on the same day every month. They need to cash the check and deposit it into their own account. What they do with the money after that does not matter. They can return the money to you or put it aside in a special money fund. The important fundamental here is that you are establishing the best rent history possible. Whether you attend college, live at home or get an apartment out of High School, be aware of rental history. Make sure this is a priority payment, so as to avoid any 30-day late charges.

The fourth step is to eventually start an installment loan, such as a car or a school loan, again pay by check consistently on the same day each month. The installment loan shows you have borrowed "X" amount of dollars, and by paying steady monthly payments on time you will have successfully paid off the loan over a set period of time. All these payments affect your credit FICO score, which I will discuss later in this chapter.

Understanding Late Payments

Late payments can be a common problem among some individuals and couples. There are basically three reasons for late payments:
1. You don't realize (understand) that paying late affects your credit.
2. You may think you have no options besides making the payment late.
3. You make a double payment one month and don't realize you're still obligated to make a payment the following month.

Late payments will cause you to pay a "late fee" but more critical your credit is affected negatively. Creditors will report the fact that your payment was not on time to credit bureaus, and this in turn will lower your credit score. Anyone who inquires about your credit value in the future will see that you made a late payment, and will see your lowered credit score.

Many creditors consider a payment late once it is received 30 or more days after the due date. They do however have the right to call your payment late one day after the due date. Never assume you are safe to pay a couple of days late. Ask your lender about the grace period and make sure you pay within that time frame.

There are three major credit reporting bureaus. They are Equifax, Experian and Trans Union. Credit bureaus compile a record of your debts and how you have repaid them. They gather information from credit card companies, department stores, banks and other firms. This information makes up your credit report. Each of these credit agencies has a file for you and your rating with them. When you make a payment on time, your lender reports to one or more of these bureaus. Conversely when you make a late payment this is also reported. Your payments will either be recorded on time, 30, 60, 90, or 120 days late. The more late payments you have and the longer you have gone without paying for them on time, the worse your overall credit score is going to be.

Always work to make your payments on time. However, it is understandable that this may not be possible in every situation. If you know that you will not be able to make a payment on time or in full, call the creditor. Let them know that you may pay late and explain the situation. Lenders can be very understanding and reasonable. Their goal is to be paid each month, not trying to destroy your credit. If you explain your situation ahead of time, they **may** be able to work with you, keeping your credit in decent shape and maybe even waive any late fees. (If you get help with your credit area, don't worry about paying the late fees). If the lender cannot or will not do anything to change your credit history (pertaining to your credit report), then you will have to work slowly and carefully to improve your credit rating. Late payments will remain on your credit for seven years or more, but they should only affect your rating for one or two years.

Do **NOT** assume that overpaying or paying twice in one month will release you from your obligation to pay the following month. Most lenders want one payment every month for the amount in question, they don't care how much extra you prepaid the month prior, or how many extra payments you make. I suggest you consult each lender to find out their policy on making extra monthly payments. (I will discuss making extra principal payments on a home in Chapter 5).

Source: Alternative Mortgage Solutions, Crestwood, Missouri

Your Credit Report and FICO Score

You establish credit history if you have ever borrowed money for a major purchase or used a major credit card. This information is stored in computers at the three credit bureaus I discussed earlier. Your credit score, often called a FICO score (after the popular model developed by Fair Isaac), is the largest provider of consumer credit scoring models. Your FICO score can range from 300-850. The lower the number the worse your credit is and the higher the number the better you appear credit wise. Be aware that credit scores can determine your financial life and they are a trend of the future. They will determine the interest rate on your home loan and credit card, the premium on your auto/home insurance, as well as your worthiness as a tenant. Each of the major credit bureaus (Equifax, Experian and TransUnion) creates its own proprietary score, as well as it's own FICO score. Let's take a look at how credit scores influence creditors in four industries: mortgages, auto loans, credit cards and auto/home insurance.

Mortgages

When you apply for a mortgage, most lenders will pull your FICO score from each of the three credit bureaus and use the median score to determine the interest rate you will pay. Most of the lenders say that a score above 620 is considered creditworthy, while a 670 score or higher is excellent. In an example for a 30 year fixed $200,000 mortgage, a score of 675 would have gotten you a rate of 6.4% interest rate. But if you had a score of 720 your rate would be 5.7%, a difference of $10,320 in loan payments over 10 years.

Auto Loans

Auto loans are much like those for mortgages, both in the way they're calculated and the way lenders use them. Lenders seem to raise their standards yearly but even a few points can make a difference. An example: for a 48 month auto loan in Missouri a credit score of 730 would have earned you a 4.96% interest rate; a credit score of 700 gets you a 6.4% interest rate.

Credit Cards

Almost all credit card companies use FICO scores, the same score the mortgage lenders use, to determine the interest rate you'll pay. There are no established guidelines for what the credit card industry considers an ideal rate, each company sets its own standards. These rates can fluctuate from quarter to quarter. Many credit card companies have you sign contracts that allow them to check on your credit report periodically. For example if they see you have recently taken out a home equity loan, you possibly present a greater risk of defaulting and they may raise your interest rate. If your interest rate jumps suddenly call the company to find out why.

Auto/Homeowners Insurance

Studies have shown that insurers have known the following: the better your credit history, the less likely you are to file a claim against your insurance agency policy. The reverse is true – the worse your credit history, the more likely you are to file frequent and sizable claims. Bad credit seems to put you in a specific group that is more likely to have an auto accident, compared to other groups. Your insurance score, better known as an "insurance risk score," is different from your FICO score. Because the insurance score measures your likelihood of filing a claim, insurers are looking for a track record of stability. Here again, a history of on-time bill payments is a good indicator of stability, the amount of debt you carry matters less to them. Depending upon your insurer, your driving record and the number of claims you've made against your home insurer are just as important as your credit score in determining the premium you'll pay. These factors tell the insurer the probability of your filing claims. For car insurers they look closely at your driving record, and your traffic violations, such as the common ones: speeding, running a stop sign or red light. They also look at more serious violations such as reckless driving or driving while under the influence of alcohol or drugs. On the home insurance side, many companies use loss history reports. These reports help to verify the information provided by applicants regarding their claim experience. They also help determine the claim history of the property you are looking to purchase. (Of course with a new home construction there are different factors). Since the mid-1990s, most property and casualty insurance companies have reported claim experience to three claim history exchanges. Those exchanges are ChoicePoint CLUE, A-Plus, and HITS.

Here are Factors That Make up your FICO Score

A history of on time payments. This is the biggest ingredient...35% of the total score. Creditors check this carefully, primarily to determine the likelihood of your defaulting on your mortgage in the next 90 days. Watch out for those 30, 60, 90, and 120 day late payments, they really drag your score down.

How much credit you use each month. This makes up 30% of the score. Creditors will be reviewing your balances on credit cards, how many credit cards you carry, also for any collections that are due, and judgments or bankruptcies.

Length of credit history. This accounts for 15% of your score. The longer your relationship with a creditor the better. To score higher here, don't close your old accounts even if you rarely use them. Unused credit doesn't hurt you.

Recent credit inquiries. This accounts for 10% of your score. The number of credit inquiries from lenders in recent months will be assessed, as well as too many will drag down your score. Creditors see a lot of inquiries and assume your shopping for more debt, which can be a negative.

Managing different kinds of debt. This accounts for the last 10% of your score. Lenders want to know you've had experience in making timely payments on different kinds of debt, such as a car loan, a credit card or a mortgage. If you have never bought a car, if you have a clean record of making timely payments on 3 credit cards and have kept balances below your credit limit, that's just as good.

Source: U.S. News & World Report June 2002

How to Obtain a Copy of Your Score

Get a copy of your FICO score and credit report from each of the three bureaus (Equifax, Experian, and TransUnion) because they will all differ. Credit card companies don't always report information to all three, which can influence your score. The consumer website of Fair Isaac (myfico.com) is the only place you can get FICO scores from all three agencies. The trio costs $38.85, and that includes a credit report from each bureau. It is a good decision to look at them at least once a year. If you see an error, call that bureau and dispute it.

Equifax – (1-800-685-1111)
Experian – (1-888-397-3742)
TransUnion – (1-800-888-4213)

The Internet offers many opportunities to check your scores and credit reports. Most of the score providers offer a range of services, from a one time check of a single score based on a single credit file to a year's subscription that allows you to monitor all changes in your credit data. The following are some of those sites:

Free Credit Reports for Missouri Consumers (annualcreditreport. com) You can also call 1-877-322-8228. Or you can print the form at (ftc.gov/credit) and then complete the Annual Credit Report Request Form and mail it to: Annual Credit Report Request Service, P.O. Box 105281, Atlanta, GA 30348-5281. Note: Do not contact the three nationwide consumer reporting companies individually with this offer.

MyFICO (myfico.com) This is co-sponsored by Fair Isaac and Equifax, so your Equifax credit file is the basis of this credit score. $13-$39.

Scorecard (scorecard.experian.com) Score is based on Experian data. $13-$80.

TransUnion (transunion.com) TransUnion sells credit reports under the limitations of the Fair Credit Reporting Act and state laws and tacks on no extra charge. That means you won't pay more than $9.

E-Loan (eloan.com) This Internet lender offers consumers a free credit score based on information on file with TransUnion. No credit report included.

For $12.95 you can order a copy of your home or auto insurance score from ChoicePoint at (choicetrust.com). You can get a copy of your home's claim history, the CLUE report from ChoicePoint for $9.

The exchanges can be contacted directly by telephone or Web site as follows:

Comprehensive Loss Underwriting Exchange (CLUE), 1-866-527-2600 or (choicetrust.com).

Automated Property Loss Underwriting System (A-Plus), 1-800-709-8842.

Federal Law sets procedures for correcting inaccurate information in a credit report. One of the benefits of reviewing your report online is the ability to challenge bad information by clicking on a box on the web site. After a challenge, the credit bureau has 30 days to check with the creditor who supplied the information. If the creditor agrees, the credit bureau makes the correct changes. You can also contact the creditor to pursue the issue. If the disagreement gets a little hostile you have the right to add to your credit file a statement explaining the dispute. The Federal Trade Commission, at (ftc.gov) or 877-382-4357, can advise you about your rights in a credit dispute.

Improving Your Credit Rating

You can improve your credit rating. Basically creditors decide how they will grant you credit based on the following criteria:

- **How you pay your bills**
- **The total amount you owe other creditors**
- **The amount of your annual income**
- **How long you have resided at your present address**
- **How the creditor could collect from you should you fail to repay**

Each creditor has a different system to evaluate your credit potential. They are looking to gauge your capacity to repay, your credit worthiness and your character. One creditor may approve your application while another creditor may turn you down, even though they have the basic identical information. The following are some tips to improve your credit profile:

Pay your bills on time. Remember that 35% of your credit score is based on your debt repayment history.

Pay down debt. If you're maxed out on credit cards, stop spending and work hard to pay down the balance.

Maintain long-term credit relationships. Don't cancel unused cards, especially if they're your older ones. Remember unused credit doesn't hurt you.

Don't apply for too many loans. Keep control of your spending. I recommend having 3-4 credit cards and no more.

Consider the use of collateral. Collateral is something a lender can use to pay off your loan if you do not repay. A car that you own the title on, stocks and bonds, a 401K savings plan, a house, can all be used as collateral.

Seek a professional financial planner. Ask a professional for their expert advice. Could be the best $100-$500 you ever spent.

Use extreme caution with consumer credit counseling agencies. From my experience in the mortgage industry, most lenders frown upon these types of agencies. They make the payments to your creditors stretch out even longer, they get a percentage on managing the program and sometimes this is your last attempt before bankruptcy comes knocking on your door.

Dealing with Debt

What is debt you might ask? Basically it's an obligation to pay that cannot be met. Webster's Dictionary defines it, "**debt**; something owed to another; a liability; an obligation." When you borrow money, and can't pay what you have promised then you're in debt. Many families and individuals in America are in debt. They are unable to make the monthly payments on the money they borrowed. Many people tend to borrow more money to make payments on the money they've all ready borrowed.

Keep in mind the number one cause of indebtedness for young couples is housing. They purchase a home to costly for their budget, and the house eats up a lot of cash they need to pay for other bills. Then car repairs or appliance repairs come up, they buy a brand new car or new appliance and then they go in debt trying to pay for necessities like food, clothing, housing staples, and medical expenses. Keep these two statements in mind:

If you don't borrow money, you can't go into debt!

If you don't borrow any more money, you can't go further in debt!

To live debt-free requires discipline, sacrifice, patience, budgeting and a willingness to make a decision that you will pay your bills and not incur new ones, especially if you don't have the financial resources to back them up. It's a hard thing to do!

The following are some guidelines to dealing with debt:

Admit you have a problem. The most difficult step in getting out of debt is being honest with yourself, realizing "I do have a debt problem." Look at support groups in your community, just like the Alcoholics Anonymous – many groups follow similar 12 step programs in dealing with debt.

Avoid bankruptcy. Bankruptcy is running rampant in America today. Recent changes in the laws have made it too easy to file a Chapter 13 or Chapter 7. Bankruptcy is the most difficult flaw to clean up on your credit report, and usually will remain on the report for 7-10 years. Bankruptcy should only be considered as a last resort in extreme situations.

Chapter 7 – This is primarily for people with little or no income. You may be forced to sell most of your belongings to repay creditors.

Chapter 13 – This is available if the amount of your debts is below specified dollar limits and if you have a steady job. A repayment plan is set up so that your creditors are paid directly from your salary. (Garnishment of wages).

Understand why you are in debt. You can sometimes break the debt cycle if you can figure out why you started using credit in the first place. Make a list of all your debts, carefully evaluate each one and ask yourself the reason for that loan. Is there any areas that you can make adjustments like lowering your car insurance with higher deductibles or deferring student loan payments? Sit down and review your budget profile and critique every area of spending.

Stop immediately in creating any new debt. Cut up those credit cards, all but one. Cancel your overdraft protection on your checking/ savings account and eliminate major impulse purchases – get back to following your budget!

Consult someone you trust for counsel. First thing is to ask your parents for advice. Try to find someone who does financial planning for a living or counsel with a member of your church. Talk to someone you know has good financial sense. Don't be afraid to consult a professional financial planner who has experience in dealing with debt.

Call your creditors to work out a repayment schedule. Many institutions that lend money are more than happy to work out a reasonable payment schedule. Basically they just want to be repaid, if they find that you are totally committed to meeting your obligations they most likely will be very helpful.

Make a long-term range "out of debt" plan. This is a simple but effective idea plan. Work hardest to pay off your smallest debt first, then take all the money you were paying on that bill and apply it toward the next largest one. Pay that bill off and take all the money and attack the next largest bill and follow this pattern in paying down bills. If any additional "mad" money comes your way, via gift money for your birthday from Grandma or an unexpected rebate check, apply that money toward your debts.

Be Aware of Closing Your Credit Cards

You have five credit cards each with a maximum credit limit of $2,000. Let's say you have four of those cards with a zero balance, but one card left has an outstanding $2,000 balance on it. You are thinking about closing down four of your charge cards because you rarely use them. Do not close them, and here's why: with five cards you have a $10,000 maximum credit limit total ($2,000 per card), so you have a 20% credit to debt ratio, which is not bad. This will most likely give you a good credit rating FICO score in the 650 to 720 range. If you close out the four credit cards with the zero balances and have the one remaining card with a $2,000 outstanding balance, you have a credit to debt ratio of 100%. This will drive down your FICO score, especially if you close the other four cards. **DON'T** close those credit card accounts! Just keep them open, but don't continue spending on them, or use them and pay off the balance every month. This will help protect your solid, strong FICO score. Bottom line, the higher your FICO score, the better deals and interest rates you can receive as a consumer.

Recommended books dealing with how to get out of debt include:

Rapid Debt Reduction Strategies, by John Avanzini, HIS Publishing Company.
The ABC's of Getting Out of Debt, by Garrett Sutton, Warner Business Books.

NOTES:

_____

_____

_____

_____

_____

_____

_____

_____

_____

_____

_____

_____

_____

_____

_____

_____

_____

_____

_____

_____

_____

_____

_____

_____

_____

_____

NOTES:

5

BUYING A HOUSE –
BECOMING A FIRST TIME HOME BUYER

A Quick Overview of the Home-Buying Process

Buying your first home can be a challenging and rewarding experience. The more you know about how the process works, the easier you can complete the home buying and financing portion of becoming a homeowner for the first time. The more knowledge you have about a subject the better-educated consumer you become. The following offers you a brief overview for buying a home.

To begin the home buying process, you need to determine what you can afford. A good rule of thumb is that the principal and interest payment, plus taxes and insurance, should not exceed 28% of your gross income. Some other factors affecting how much home you can afford include your debts, savings and investments. Mortgage lenders will review copies of your credit report for approval. FICO scores from the three credit bureaus (Equifax, Experian, and TransUnion) will be pulled to determine your credit worthiness.

My advice is to first find a real estate agent that you are comfortable with. An agent can work for either the seller or the buyer. I would ask the chosen agent for their help in choosing a lender, many times they have an "in-house" mortgage company connection that can easily pre-qualify you, or they have a list of preferred banks and/or mortgage companies to call for financing. (Note: agents, who have been in the business a number of years, have the experience you want on your side). Choosing the right agent can be a huge advantage. Building a trusting relationship with your real estate agent is paramount, because buying a house will be one of the biggest purchases you make in your life.

Most often, you start the house buying process by getting pre-approved for a loan. We will discuss loans later in this chapter.

Once you find a home, your agent will negotiate an offer, and when the final offer is agreed upon your real estate professional will draft a sales contract for you and the seller to sign. The final contract then goes to your lender to begin the mortgage application process. This usually takes 30-60 days. The type of loan you apply for (fixed rate, adjustable rate, balloon or others) will determine how much home you can afford. Some loans require no money down, (you need excellent credit to qualify here) while others may require 5%, 10% or 20% of the home's cost as a down payment.

During the approval process, you will have the home appraised, surveyed and inspected. Meanwhile the lender will be checking your credit history, employment, rental history, and bank deposits. The lender will also want to know where the funds for a down payment are coming from such as savings, investments, inheritance or gifts, 401K programs, etc.

Once approved by your lender, you are now full steam ahead to your closing day. Prior to closing you will receive an estimate of all closing costs. On the closing day, the sale is finalized as the title company involved has prepared the certificate of title, abstract and deed. You sign the papers and you are officially a first time homeowner.

Now, let's look at more detailed information concerning buying and financing a home as well as settlement costs and other procedures.

Role of the Real Estate Agent

The first person you will be contacting in purchasing a home is a real estate agent. A real estate agent may be able to provide you more advice on many aspects of buying a home; however, be aware there are buyer's agents and seller's agents. A seasoned real estate agent can offer you a lot from their years of experience. You will typically choose an agent from a referral or by meeting with two to three agents and de-ciding on the one you are most comfortable with. Make sure the agent you choose is knowledgeable about the community you are looking to buy in. They should know the schools, churches, businesses, shopping centers and other questions you'll have about that "living area." Ask your agent about the location, condition, and price of the homes in the area you are shopping. Ask your Realtor to offer their guidance and explanation of the competition and your pricing strategy. Your agent should be available to contact daily, a diligent worker on your behalf and be able to effectively present both positive and negative assets of each property you look at.

Selecting an Attorney

To me this is optional. Before you sign a sales contract, you might get a copy of the contract and have an attorney review it to make sure it protects your interest. Many Real Estate companies have attorney approved contracts provided. My advice is ask your real estate agent and they can help you make a decision based upon their experience in working with home sales contracts. Keep in mind there will probably be additional fees upon consulting an attorney. Always put a contingency in the contract based upon inspection, etc., as an out, thus no need for a lawyer.

Terms of the Sales Contract

Keep in mind when working with a sales contract you can make changes or additions to the form agreement, but the seller must agree to every change you make. You need to also agree with the seller on your move in date, what appliances etc., and other property, such as curtains, ceiling fans, hot tub, that with be sold with the home. Your real estate agent will help you negotiate the sales contract.

Sales Price – For most home buyers, the sales price is the most important term. Many times you make an initial offer on price and then the seller may counter that offer. Here again your Realtor will help you in the negotiating matters.

Title – The title refers to the legal ownership of your new home. The seller should provide a title, clear and free of all claims by others against your new home. A title search will be requested on behalf of the lender, so they know there are no "liens" or "encumbrances" against the house they are lending on. The owner's title policy is very important, make sure this is done properly and correctly!

Mortgage Clause – The sales contract should provide this clause that your deposit will be returned if the sale has to be canceled because you are unable to get proper financing. You could cancel the contract if you cannot obtain mortgage financing at an interest rate at or below a rate you specify in the sales contract.

Pests – Your lender might require a certificate from a qualified inspector stating the home is free from termites and other pests or pest damage.

Home Inspection – It is a recommended procedure to have a home building inspection done. (Use as a contingency in the contract). This inspection should determine the condition of the plumbing, heating, cooling and electrical systems. The structure should also be examined to determine the condition of the roof, siding, doors and windows. Most contracts state that the buyer pays for this inspection so that the inspector is working for them, not the seller. If you are not satisfied with the inspection results, you may want to re-negotiate for a lower price or require the seller to make repairs. Most inspectors are a member of the American Society of Home Inspectors (ASHI). For more information look at (ashi.com).

Municipality Home Inspection – Many local communities require their own community housing inspection. The seller typically covers this cost, and the city inspector will determine that all the city rules and regulations are met for the overall condition of the home, inside and outside. Every municipality has their own set of guidelines.

Lead-Based Paint Hazards in Housing built before 1978 – If you buy a home built before 1978, you have certain rights concerning lead-based paint and lead poisoning hazards. Check with your agent on how this may affect your sales contract and that the seller must disclose any information they know pertaining to lead-based paint hazards.

Sharing of Expenses – You need to agree with the seller about how expenses related to property taxes, water, sewer charges, condominium fees, and utility bills are to be divided on the day of closing. As a buyer, you should only be responsible for the portion of these expenses owed after the date of the sale.

Settlement Agent/Title Company – Depending upon local practices you may have an option to select the closing agent or title closing company.

Settlement Costs – You can negotiate which settlement costs you will pay and what the seller will pay on their behalf. Depending upon the type of loan you qualify for and the particular lender, you can ask for help from the buyer to have them pay a portion of the closing costs. Ask you Realtor to help you identify these areas.

Shopping for a Loan

As you decide which type of loan will best suit your needs, the lender and type of loan will affect your settlement costs and also the monthly costs of your new home mortgage loan. There are many different lenders and types of loans you can choose from. In this chapter I want to familiarize you with some of your options. You may shop a loan from banks, savings associations, credit unions and mortgage companies. Many of them are listed in the yellow pages, the local newspaper, as well as on TV and the Internet. My advice is ask family and friends for referrals first. That is the better way to start. The next best option depending upon your situation is your bank where you have your checking account. Let's look at some options:

- **Government Loans** – You may be eligible for a loan insured through the Federal Housing Administration (FHA) or guaranteed by the Department of Veterans Affairs (VA). These programs usually require a small down payment, usually 3-5%. For more information on government loans contact the following:
- **FHA** – Insured home mortgage loans on one to four family dwellings, call 1-800-225-5342.
- **VA** – Programs offered by the Department of Veterans Affairs, if you are a veteran or qualify by military service contact your nearest VA Regional Office @ 800-827-1000 or web site (va.gov.vas.loan).
- **U.S. Department of Housing and Urban Development** – Call 1-800-767-4483 or web site (hud.gov).

CLOs – Computer loan origination systems, or CLOs, are computer terminals sometimes available in real estate offices or other locations that help you review the various types of loans offered by different lenders. The CLO operator may charge a fee for services, and the fee may be paid by you or the lender that you select.

Banks, Savings Associations & Credit Unions – There are many choices here, of course the bank where you have your checking account is the first place to shop. Depending upon the guidelines, certain Savings Associations and Credit Unions, if you can meet their prescribed criteria, offer excellent programs with reduced costs/rates for their members.

Mortgage Brokers – These companies offer to find you a mortgage lender willing to make you a loan. If you have less than perfect credit, mortgage brokers usually have over 50 or more different lenders they can do business with to help you secure the right loan that fits your current situation. Your mortgage broker may be paid by the lender, you the borrower or both. Ask the mortgage broker about the fees they charge for their services. A mortgage broker with experience will definitely work hard on your behalf. Check out the company, how many years the loan officer has been in the business and what advice they give you on the first initial call.

The following is a sample of some of the programs lenders can offer:

104% Loans – This includes your down payment and closing costs. No down payment is required and most of your closing costs are wrapped into the loan.

100% Loans – No down payment required, but remember you have closing costs to deal with. Sometimes you can negotiate to have the seller pay up to 3% of closing costs.

97% Loans – Requires only 3% down payment, seller can contribute to closing costs.

FHA Loan – Government backed loan requires only 3% down payment.

VA Loan – Military Loan if you have served your country, usually requiring smaller 3-5% down payment.

80/20 Purchase Loan – No down payment is required. Here you actually get two loans, the first mortgage 80% loan will be at a going rate (with no PMI) and the second mortgage 20% loan will have a much higher rate depending upon the lender.

80/15/5 Purchase Loan – This loan has you putting a 5% down payment, getting a first mortgage 80% loan at a going rate (with no PMI) and then securing a second mortgage 15% loan for a higher interest rate depending upon the lender.

No Income Verification – This loan requires no proof of income, you give a stated income amount and light documentation if you have high FICO scores and maybe own your own business, this can be an option although you will have slightly higher interest rates.

NINA Loan – This loan (No Income No Assets) requires no proof of income, no proof of assets, light documentation and can work well for the independent business owner.

30-Year Fixed Loan – Loan has a fixed interest rate for 30 years. (Standard in the industry). This loan is also available on a 25 year fixed interest rate, usually same rate applies.

20-Year Fixed Loan – Loan has a fixed interest rate for 20 years, interest rate should be lower that a 30-year interest rate.

15-Year Fixed Loan – This loan has a fixed interest rate for 15 years, also available in a 10 year fixed rate.

3-Year ARM Loan – This loan is an adjustable rate mortgage, meaning that for the first three years you can get a lower interest rate than normal, after three years it adjusts by margins, usually cannot go over more than 2% a year and for the life of the loan it will not exceed 4%.

5-Year ARM Loan – This loan is an adjustable rate mortgage also, only the term for the lower interest rate is 5 years.

30/15 Year Balloon Loan – This loan has a set interest rate for 15 years, and at the end of that term the remaining full amount of the loan is due and payable in one lump sum.

Other Specialty Programs

-Credit Blending Programs   -No FICO Score Programs
-Programs with No PMI   -Programs with No Reserves
-Programs with No Seasoning   -Self-Employed Programs
-Tandem Loan Programs   -Neighborhood Grant Programs

Types of Loans

There are basically two types of loans, one being a fixed interest rate and the other a variable interest rate. Fixed rate loans have the same principal and interest payments during the loan term. Variable rate loans, also known as an adjustable rate mortgage (ARM) can have any number of "indexes" and "margins" which determine how and when the rate and payment amount will change. Depending upon the index and the margin, most ARM products can't exceed above 2% in a year period and will not go beyond 5% over the life of the loan. Most loans can be repaid over a term of 30 years or less and most loans have equal monthly payments. Balloon loans have short terms and then one large final payment at the end of that term.

Understanding Interest Rate, Points and Other Fees

Many times the price of a home mortgage loan is stated in terms of an interest rate, points, and other fees. You can select some interest rates that have no points (extra fee) associated with them. A "point" is a fee that equals 1% of the loan amount. Points are usually paid to the lender, the mortgage broker, or both at the settlement or upon the completion of the escrow. Many times, you can pay more points for a lower interest rate. For example you might be able to get a 6% interest rate on a 30 year fixed loan from a lender with no points. But if you pay 1 point you would be able to obtain a 5.75% interest rate on the same 30 year fixed loan. My suggestion is try to get the lowest interest rate without having to pay any points. (Spend or save that "points" money for other needs). You need to ask your lender or mortgage broker about points and extra fees.

A document known as the Truth in Lending Disclosure Statement will show you "Annual Percentage Rate" (APR) and other payment information on the loan you have applied for. The APR takes into account not only the interest rate, but also the mortgage broker fees, points and other fees you have to pay for. It is a good idea to ask for the APR before you apply to help you shop for the loan that is best for you. Also inquire if your loan has a special fee for paying all or part of the loan off early, known as a prepayment penalty. You may be able to negotiate the terms of the prepayment penalty, depending upon the type of loan you obtain. Note: The worse your credit FICO scores, many ARM products you look at **WILL** have prepayment penalties. **Note**: Check with your lender/broker when you have your initial RESPA meeting and clarify about whether your loan has a prepayment penalty. Most loans for A and A- borrowers do not have prepay penalties. The option here is that you will be able to pay the loan off early before the term period and thus be able to save "mucho dinero" on the interest. If you win the lottery or get a sudden inheritance and choose to pay off the home you can do it. Not having a house payment is a nice thing, and it reduces stress levels.

Be aware that points can usually be deducted for the tax year that you purchase a house, which may affect how you shop for a loan. One key decision in purchasing your first home is how long do you plan to stay in the home. The national average for most first time home buyers is about 5 years. If you have a pretty good idea you will be moving in 3-5 years I suggest looking at an ARM product. This gives you the best interest rate and lowest payment to start out in buying your first home.

Lender Required Settlement Costs

Your lender may require you to obtain specific settlement services. These may include a new survey of the property, mortgage insurance or title insurance. You may have to order and get charged for other settlement related services, such as fees for a credit report, and a house appraisal. Some lenders have fees for loan processing, documentation preparation, flood certification, underwriting, or an application fee. I recommend asking for an estimate of fees and settlement costs before choosing a lender or mortgage broker. Be very careful if a mortgage broker has points, as well as broker fees or loan origination fees. Sometimes these can be avoided by shopping at least 3 different lenders and getting an estimate of their closing costs and settlement fees. Be aware that some lenders offer "no costs" or "no point" loans, they are usually covering their costs or fees by charging a higher interest rate. Later in this chapter we will cover more on settlement charges.

Understanding about "Locking In" Your Rate

Interest rates change on a daily basis, sometimes they can adjust up or down throughout the day. Keep in mind that starting a loan process can take from 30-45 days and sometimes longer depending upon the hurdles you have to go through with the lender, the appraisal, the house inspection, city inspection, etc. "Locking in" your rate or points at the time of application or during the process of your loan will keep the rate and/or points from changing until you reach the closing date of your home loan. Ask your lender or broker if there is a fee to lock-in the rate and whether the fee reduces the amount you have to pay for points. Generally, most lenders don't have a lock-in fee. Find out how long the lock-in is good for, some rates can be locked for 30, 45 and even 60 days. Also ask whether the lock-in fee is refundable should your application be rejected. Here is where a good, seasoned broker works with you carefully in explaining the current interest rate situation; he should have some knowledge of whether rates may be climbing, going down, or staying the same.

Understanding Mortgage Insurance (Also known as PMI)

Private Mortgage Insurance and government mortgage insurance protect the lender against default (your failure to make continued home payments – thus you lose your home), and enable the lender to make a loan, which the lender considers a higher risk.

Lenders often require mortgage insurance (PMI) for loans where the downpayment is less than 20% of the sales price. Most lenders bill monthly for your mortgage insurance premium. Ask your lender if mortgage insurance is required and how much it will cost.

Some 100% loans do not have PMI, reflecting a higher interest rate depending upon your FICO score. In each specific case, you have to be aware that PMI will be an additional fee onto your monthly home loan, including your principal and interest payment, on top of your homeowner's insurance and real estate taxes. See an example below:

A loan of $90,000 at 6.5% rate with 10% down payment to purchase a home for $100,000 (excluding your closing costs) would look like this:

Principal & Interest	$568.86	
Real Estate Taxes	$104.00	($1250/year)
Homeowner's Insurance	$ 50.00	($600/year)
PMI	$ 39.00	($468/year)
Total	$761.86	

Important Note: Do not confuse mortgage insurance (PMI) with mortgage life or credit life insurance, which are designed to pay off a mortgage in the event of the borrower's death or disability. **I DO NOT** recommend purchasing home mortgage insurance to pay off your house in case you die. You should invest in a life insurance program and use part of this money to pay off your house should you or your spouse becomes deceased.

Additional Items to Consider

Tax and Insurance payments – Your monthly mortgage payment will be used to repay the money you borrowed plus interest. As stated above you also have real estate taxes and homeowner's insurance to add to that payment. I highly recommend that you work with the lender to set up an "escrow account" also known as a reserve or impound account. Have your insurance and taxes included in your monthly house payment. Money is collected in advance at the time of closing to set up this escrow account. Usually 12 months of homeowners insurance is paid before or at closing and depending upon the time of the year you close you will have an adjusted charge for your real estate taxes. This money is put into the escrow account so the lender has the money to pay your taxes and insurance (and flood insurance) when they are due. In Missouri, real estate taxes are due to be paid end of the year on or before December 31.

Flood Hazard Insurance – Most lenders will not lend you money to buy a home in a flood hazard area unless you pay for flood insurance. Your lender usually has a small fee, around $10 to $25, to check the home you are buying to make sure it is not in a designated flood area. You will be notified if flood insurance is required. Also be aware that if a change in flood insurance maps brings your home within a flood area after your loan is made, your lender may require you to buy flood insurance at that time. **Note**: Flood insurance is not **CHEAP**! Be prepared to pay some extra monthly dollars for this insurance.

Transfer of your loan – Keep in mind that while you may start the loan process with one lender or mortgage broker, you could find another company collecting the payments on your loan not too far down the road. Many times loans are sold and acquired by another lender, called a loan transfer. At the time of closing your lender or broker will disclose whether it expects to service the loan or share the percentage of your loan being transferred (sold) to someone else. But don't worry, your monthly payment will be the same, your principal and interest payment remain constant, but you can have adjustments in your taxes, insurance, PMI and maybe flood insurance.

Determining An Affordable Mortgage

Before you begin shopping for your future home you need to have a good idea of how much mortgage payment you can afford each month. A good rule of thumb is that the principal and interest payment, plus taxes and insurance, should not exceed 28 percent of your gross income. Another formula to use includes if your principal and interest payment, plus taxes and insurance and all debt, does not exceed 36 percent then you can multiply your current gross income by .36 to determine your maximum monthly mortgage payment. See my examples below:

Figuring for principal and interest payment, plus taxes and insurance only:

Your monthly income	$_____
Multiplied by .28	x .28
Recommended maximum monthly payment =	$_____

Figuring for principal and interest payment, plus taxes and insurance and all debt:

Your monthly income	$_____
Multiplied by .36	x.36
Recommended maximum monthly payment =	$_____

Sources you can use for a Down Payment

Inheritance Money – Need a letter signed by parent or grandparent stating this is an inheritance they are giving you, no seasoning required-put in the checking account ASAP.

Gift of Equity – Money from family or friends, requires 60-180 days of seasoning, so that means this money must be sitting in your checking/savings account for 60-180 days, depending upon the lender and their requirements.

Savings Account or Money Market Account – Usually you have this money saved aside to use to purchase a house. If this money has been accruing in your account 60 to 180 days, most lenders will work within these time frames.

401K Program – Most businesses allow you to take a portion or all of your 401K account and apply that money toward a first time home buyer down payment. 401K programs all follow their own guidelines and rules, check with your company 401K sponsor.

Charitable Organization Gifts – Contact your broker or lender on these various programs that offer first time home buying assistance, money toward some down payment and/or closing cost.

Be Creative – As a mortgage consultant, I once worked to help refinance a lady named Shelly. Here is a great story of how two sisters worked together, pooling their money resources to buy a house. Shelly and her sister Debbie, after getting some great advice from their parents, decided that by pooling together the money they saved, the two had $10,000 to use as a down payment for a house. They bought a home with each of their names on the title. And they lived together for 6+ years. After that time, Debbie decided she was ready to get married to her boyfriend and move out. Shelly called me at the mortgage company to refinance her loan and have her sister's name removed from the title. She needed to do a "cash-out" refinance loan, to pay off Debbie's investment in the home. They initially bought the home for $85,000, but now with increased appraisal value of the home it appraised for $135,000. Shelly was able to lower her interest rate and take out $24,000 to pay off her sister and still have a reasonable house payment, one she could afford as a single woman. This is a terrific story of creative financing to become a homeowner, especially for a single person.

Items Required to Process Your Loan

What do I need to bring to apply for a loan you might ask! The following is a general list of items you will need to gather to proceed with the processing and closing of your loan in a timely manner. When you first meet with a lender or broker these are the most common things you will be asked to bring.

- Copies of your last 2 years W-2s.
- Copies of your last Federal Tax return.
- Copies of your most recent pay stubs.
- Landlord information-will need to verify the last two years rental history.
- Copies of your 2 most recent checking/savings account statements (all pages are required).
- Copies of your most recent investment statement (401K, IRA, CD, etc.).
- Complete copy of divorce decree, if applicable.
- Copy of the Sales Contract for the home you are buying.
- Homeowner's insurance information (agents name and telephone number).
- Copy of earnest money check (front and back).
- Completed and signed credit authorization.
- Completed and signed mortgage loan application.
- Other:_____

Determining Monthly Income Calculations

One part of the loan application process will ask you for your monthly income, the following are helpful calculations to answer these questions:

Hourly Pay X 40 X 52 divided by 12 = Monthly Pay
Weekly Pay X 52 divided by 12 = Monthly Pay
Bi-Weekly Pay X 26 divided by 12 = Monthly Pay
Semi-Monthly Pay X 2 = Monthly Pay

RESPA Disclosures

RESPA (Real Estate Settlement Procedures Act) is a federal law that requires the lender to provide home mortgage borrowers with information of known or estimated settlement costs. RESPA requires that borrowers receive disclosures at various times. RESPA also limits the amount lenders may require to be held in escrow account for real estate taxes and insurance, requires the disclosure of known settlement costs of both the buyers and sellers by the person conducting the settlement, and outlaws certain referral fees.

Good Faith Estimate of Settlement Costs. RESPA requires that when you apply for a loan, the lender or mortgage broker give you a Good Faith Estimate (GFE) of settlement service charges you will likely have to pay. If you do not get this GFE when you apply for a loan, the mortgage broker or lender must mail or deliver to you within the next three business days. Remember that the amounts listed on the GFE are estimates only, the actual costs may vary and that the lender's estimate is not a guarantee. I recommend you keep your GFE so you can compare it with the final settlement costs and ask your broker or lender about any changes.

Servicing Disclosure Statement. RESPA requires the mortgage broker or lender to tell you in writing, when you apply for a loan or within the next three business days, whether it expects that someone else will be servicing your loan.

HUD-1 Settlement Statement. One business day before the settlement or closing date, you have the right to inspect the HUD-1 Settlement Statement. In most cases, the mortgage broker or lender calls you via phone to tell you what the final HUD-1 settlement costs are and what the final dollar figure will be, so you know the exact amount for the cashier check to come to closing with. Ask the lender or broker to fax you the final HUD-1 so you can review and check numbers with your GFE. Not everything will be as it was on the GFE, but is should be close. Ask questions if you have them.

Escrow Account Operation & Disclosures. Most lenders will require an escrow account to be established, to insure that your taxes and insurance premiums are paid on time. You will have to pay an initial amount at the settlement to start the account and an additional amount with each month's payment. Your escrow account payments may include a "cushion" or extra amount to insure the lender has enough money to make the payments when they are due. RESPA limits the amount of the "cushion" to a maximum of two months of escrow payments, no more than this.

Understanding Your Closing Costs

If you have a good understanding of what to expect for your settlement costs it will help you be an educated consumer. When shopping for closing costs you can use this section simply as a guideline. With many lenders to choose from you will have different fees quoted by service providers (banks, credit unions, brokers) and the closing costs can increase the cost of your loan so compare carefully. Let's look at some the fees associated with settlement charges. Please note that not all these fees will be on a closing statement, but the more you are aware of certain fees the more knowledgeable you will be.

Mortgage Broker Fee. This is usually an additional fee the mortgage broker might charge you if you have less then worthy credit. Something to watch for and if you see this fee ask the broker **WHY** has he included it.

Loan Origination Fee. This fee is usually known as a loan origination fee, but sometimes is called a point or points. It covers the lender's administrative cost in processing the loan. This fee will vary, as often it is expressed as a percentage of the loan. Some brokers include it as an "add-on" fee. Be careful here to look closely at any origination fee.

Loan Discount or Points Fee. This is known as points, the loan discount is a one-time charge imposed by the lender or broker to lower the rate at which they would otherwise offer the loan to you. Each "point" is equal to one percent of the mortgage amount. An example – if a lender charges 2 points on a $100,000 loan this amounts to a charge of $2000.

Appraisal Fee. This charge pays for an appraisal report made by a certified appraiser to determine the sales value of the home. The fee usually ranges from $300 to $500. Make sure at closing you get a **COPY** of your appraisal report.

Credit Report Fee. This fee covers the cost of pulling your credit history with the three credit bureaus we discussed in Chapter 4. The lender uses this credit report information to decide whether or not to approve your loan and how much money to lend you. This fee should range from $15 to $30.

Processing Fee. This fee can covers the cost of the processing team that works to process all your paperwork. This fee should range from $250 to $450.

Documentation Fee. This fee can be an added-on charge; this covers processing of all the documents and/or paperwork. Be careful here, you should have either a processing fee or a documentation fee, not both. This fee should range from $100 to $300.

Underwriting Fee. This fee can be charged by various lenders for their paper processing and administrative team costs. This fee should range from $200 to $500. **Note**: You should not see all three together on a closing statement; Processing/Documentation/Underwriting charges.

Wire Transfer Fee. This fee is charged for wiring money from the title company or sometimes the appraiser. Usually you do not see this fee. Might range from $25 to $50.

Courier Fee. This fee is a charge for the courier cost to deliver all your paperwork to/and from the lender for final approval. This fee should range from $25 to $50.

Lender's Inspection Fee. This charge covers inspections, often of newly constructed housing, made by employees of your lender or by an outside inspector.

Assumption Fee. This is a fee which is charged when a buyer assumes or takes over the duty to pay the seller's existing mortgage loan. Not very common any more, these were called assumable loans and they rarely exist today.

Interest. Lenders usually require borrowers to pay the interest that accrues from the date of settlement to the first monthly payment. Look for this on the HUD-1 statement.

Mortgage Insurance Premium. The lender may require you to pay your first year's mortgage insurance premium, or a lump sum premium that covers the life of the loan, in advance, at the closing. I recommend not buying Mortgage Insurance.

Hazard Insurance Premium. Also known as homeowner's insurance, protects you and the lender against loss due to fire, windstorm and natural hazards. Lenders often require the borrower to bring to closing a paid-up first year's policy (or your insurance agent can fax the paid receipt in) or to pay for the first year's premium at closing. Because of Insurance companies and different rating programs, they have their own guidelines. You will be best to shop for homeowner's insurance. Range from $300/year and up.

Flood Insurance Premium. If the lender requires flood insurance, it is usually paid-up one year in advance, similar to your homeowner's insurance. This insurance will also be costly, contact your homeowner agent and get their help in estimating costs here.

Home Inspection Fee. This is paid outside of closing, where you the borrower should pay to have an independent licensed home inspector come out to look at the property reviewing electrical, plumbing, HVAC, structural, etc. This fee can range from $250 to $500.

Local Municipality Inspection. This fee should usually be covered by the seller, and if there are any repairs required to meet housing codes for that municipality the seller pays these fees. This fee can range from $30 to $125.

The following are **Title Company** related charges, they may cover a variety of services performed by the title companies and others. Your particular settlement statement may not include all of the items listed below or may include others not listed.

Notary Fee. This fee is charged for the cost of having a person who is licensed as a notary public swear to the fact that the persons named in the documents did sign them. This fee is around $15 to $25.

Attorney's Fees. You may be required to pay for legal services provided to the lender, such as an examination of the title binder. Sometimes the seller will agree to pay part of this fee. Sometimes this fee is not included. (State specific)

Title Closing Fee. This is the fee charged for services by the title company itself. This fee should range from $150 to $350.

Title Insurance. The total cost of the owner's and lender's title insurance. This fee should range from $350 and up depending upon the sale price of the home.

Owner's Title Insurance. The fee here is for the cost of the owner's policy which provides an insurance policy insuring past title evidence. Title insurance insures free and clear ownership rights.

Government Recording Fees. The buyer usually pays the fees for legally recording the new deed and mortgage at the recorder of deeds office.

Survey. The lender may require that a surveyor conduct a property survey. Sometimes an old survey can be used, and usually the buyer pays the surveyor's fee, but sometimes the seller pays this. There can be a stake survey, spot survey or actual land survey, depending upon if the lender requires a survey. Fees will start at $125 and go up.

Courier Fee. This is a fee charge for courier service to deliver the documents to the lender. The fee should range from $25 to $50.

Pest/Termite Inspection Fee. This fee is to cover inspection for termites and other pest infestation of your home. This fee should range from $50 to $100.

Lead-Based Paint Inspection Fee. This fee is to cover inspections or evaluations for lead-based paint hazard risk assessments and may or may not be needed.

Flood Letter. By government regulations there will need to be a letter of Flood Certification to state that the house you are buying is not in a flood plain. Fee for this service is usually $10 to $25.

So as we look at our estimated closing costs to buy our first home (not including a down payment), I would propose fees ranging from $2500 to $3800 based upon a sales price of a home in the $150,000 to $250,000 price range. Estimates for closing costs could range from 1% to 3% of the selling price of the home.

Understanding What Type of Borrower You Are

There are five basic types of borrowers. They are generally known as A, A-, B, C, and D.

A Borrowers – They have excellent credit and usually qualify for the best conventional rate available. They have 3 or more trade lines on their credit, and are not exceeding their high credit balance limit. The have no late payments, collections or bankruptcies. They also have a full 2-year rent history with no late payments. An A borrower has had only one or two jobs in the past 2+ years, and they have worked in the same career field. They have a debt to income (DTI) ratio less than 38%, and a steady average balance in their bank account. Their bank accounts generally have enough reserve money to cover at least one month of their mortgage payment. A borrowers are prime candidates for higher loan to value loans.

A- Borrowers – They have good credit and will receive a rate 1-2% higher than an A borrower and will also qualify for high LTV's. They have had a couple of isolated credit problems in the past, maybe a late payment on rent, but no major credit problems like bankruptcies, fore-closures, or judgments. They also have a good rent history, with maybe one late payment, which is not more than 30 days late. They have a 2-year job history with no gaps in employment. Their debt to income ratio is generally less than 45%, and they usually have a bank account that may or may not carry a steady balance from month to month.

B and C Borrowers – They are very similar and it is hard to tell them apart, and they will get a rate about 2-4% greater than prime and still have a chance for high LTV's. However the chances are more remote for the high LTV areas. They usually have less than perfect credit and some problems with paying their monthly bills on time. They may have had a bankruptcy over 2 years ago and some paid judgments. They could have some accounts that have been placed with a collec-tion agency. They may or may not have a rent history. Their job his-tory may not be solid and they may have some periods of no employ-ment. Their DTI ratio could be as high as 50%, and they may not have any bank accounts. Depending upon each individual situation, the borrower could qualify for only a 75-90% LTV. But in some cases, through first time home buyer programs, they possibly may receive 100% financing. **Note:** Most B & C borrowers, if they get a 100% loan, will have 2-7 year prepayment penalties, depending upon what type of loan they qualify for.

D Borrowers – They have more extensive credit problems, and can expect rates 3-6% higher than prime and may have problems getting a loan for more than 75% LTV. These borrowers may have foreclosures, bankruptcies, judgments and or collections. They usually have a poor rent record or may not have one at all. Their job history may have gaps and may not be in the same line of work. Their DTI ratio could be 55% or higher, and only sometimes do they have a bank account. De-pending upon the borrower and their circumstances, however severe, this person may only qualify for 60-80% LTV. In rare cases, the LTV could go as high as 90%.

Source: Alternative Mortgage Solutions, Crestwood, Missouri

Understanding Terminology Before Buying a Home

The language of home buying has some unique terms that you probably have not come across before in your life, but as you begin the process it will be good information to have. I want you to have some basic knowledge of what these words mean and how they play a role in dealing with the real estate agent, the broker/lender and the title closing company. The following terms should help you speak the lingo:

Accrued Interest. The interest earned for the period of time that elapsed since interest was last paid.

Adjustable Rate Mortgage (ARM). A type of mortgage loan where the interest rate changes periodically up or down, usually once or twice a year.

Amortization. Gradual debt reduction. Normally, the reduction is made according to a predetermined schedule for installment payments.

Amortization Schedule. A table showing the amounts of principal and interest due at regular intervals, and the unpaid balance of the loan after each payment is made.

Annual Percentage Rate (APR). Everything financed in your mortgage loan package (interest, loan fees, points or other charges) expressed as a percentage of the loan amount.

Appraisal. A professional judgment report done by an appraiser of the value of real estate based upon knowledge, experience, and a study or other pertinent data.

Closing Day. The conclusion of a transaction. In real estate, closing includes the delivery of a deed, financial adjustments, the signing of notes, and the disbursement of funds necessary to the sale or loan transaction.

Debt to Income Ratio (DTI). The relationship between the amount of your gross monthly income and the house payment plus all debt expressed as a percentage of your income ratio. To determine take total debt including your new house payment divided into your gross monthly income.

Deed. A formal written instrument by which title to real property is transferred from one owner to another.

Down Payment. The amount of money to be paid by the purchaser to the seller upon the signing of the agreement of sale. The difference between the sales price of real estate and the mortgage amount.

Earnest Money. A sum of money given to (1) bind a sales of real estate, or (2) assure payment or an advance of funds in the processing of a loan; deposit.

Escrow. Funds paid by one party to another (the escrow agent) to hold until the occurrence of a specified event, after which the funds are released to a designated individual.

Loan to Value ratio (LTV). The relationship between the amount of the mortgage loan and the appraised value of the security expressed as a percentage of the appraised value. To determine LTV, take amount of your loan and divide it into sales price of the home.

Private Mortgage Insurance (PMI). A charge paid by the borrower (usually part of the closing costs) to obtain financing, especially when making a down payment of less than 20 percent of the purchase price.

Points. 1 percent of the amount of the mortgage loan. For example if the loan is for $50,000, one point is $500.

Property Taxes. Taxes (based on the assessed value of the home) paid by the homeowner for community services such as schools, public works and other local government costs.

Principal, Interest, Taxes and Insurance (PITI). The principal and interest of the loan amount along with your taxes and insurance.

Refinancing. The process of the same mortgage holder paying off one loan with the proceeds from another loan.

Title. As generally used, the rights of ownership and possession of a particular property (e.g., liens, etc.). In the case of real estate, the documentary evidence of ownership is the title deed, which specifies in whom the legal estate is vested and the history of ownership and transfers.

Title Insurance. Protects the lenders or homeowners against loss of their interest in property due to legal defects in title.

To look up any other terms you might have a question on go to FannieMae's website, (fanniemae.com) and click on Tools & Resources. Search for terms.

10 Final Tips When Looking to Buy Your First Home

1. Remember there are three things that must be right in buying that first home...and they are **Location/Location/Location**. If you have a tight budget and start out buying a cheaper home, at least buy it in the best location possible. Try to buy in a area where most of the houses are more expensive than yours, because their higher value will tend to drive up the value on your home. Ask your real estate agent to help with location.

2. Make sure *your credit is in good shape*. Too many times as a broker I had a number of buyers apply for a mortgage loan, knowing they had credit problems, while keeping their fingers crossed that their credit would qualify them for a loan. **WRONG!** Get your credit history in decent shape before you apply for a loan. It will save you heartache and heartbreak when you think you are ready to buy a home and your credit won't back you up. Check your credit report and FICO scores a couple months before looking to buy your first dream house.

3. Be sure to *look at first-time home buyer programs*. Many are sponsored by state, county or city governments and offer better interest rates and terms than you would find with the normal lenders and brokers. Talk to your bank and also call housing agencies for your state, county, and city to see what they offer.

4. Work to *get pre-approved for a loan*. Don't confuse being "pre-qualified" with being "pre-approved." The pre-qualification process is an estimate where a lender tells you how much money you probably can borrow based on how much money you make, where you stand on debt ratio, and how much cash you have for a down payment. But when you get pre-approval, the process has you actually applying for a loan with a lender or broker. You submit your rent history, tax returns, pay stubs along with other information. The lender verifies the information and checks your credit. When all is said and done, the lender agrees in writing to make the loan. Home sellers and their agents look very favorably at buyers who are pre-approved with a loan to back them up. Just being "pre-qualified" doesn't carry the weight that "pre-approved" does.

5. Take the time to understand what will be *the best loan program for your individual needs*. Talk to your friends, family and rela-

tives to get their advice. Then shop around at three or four lenders/brokers. Look carefully at FHA loans and other low down payment loans if that is the path you want to take. Talk to your real estate agent, as someone who has selling experience they can help you evaluate the type of real estate and loan program that will best suit your needs.

6. Make *a wish list of what you want for your first home*. Sit down and consider how long you plan to live in the house; write down goals for location, type of house, school districts, neighborhoods, shopping districts, restaurants, yardwork, swimming pool, and proximity to where you work. All these factors contribute to the type of real estate and location that will best suit your personal goals.

7. Don't *over-extend yourself with too big of a house payment.* Many people take out the largest loan they possibly can, hoping their income will increase eventually to make their house payment comfortable. First-time home buyers don't realize how expensive home ownership can be. Renting vs. owning a home is very different. You now spend more money for property taxes and homeowner's insurance, as well as higher bills for utilities, maintenance and repairs that you did as a renter. Be smart...instead of going to the brink of eating peanut butter & jelly for weeks, along with a steady diet of macaroni & cheese, consider limiting your (PITI) or housing costs to 25% or so of your gross income. It's a much more comfortable level to deal with than the 33% lenders are typically willing to give you.

8. Be careful on *paying junk fees*. Lenders can increase their profits by adding on a variety of fees. Most are legitimate, but some can be inflated while others may be pure profit. For example, they may charge $75 for a credit check that cost them $15. Look carefully at "documentation preparation," these charges will vary all over the place, and basically it involves having a computer print out the forms. Don't challenge junk fees at the closing table, it's too late! You should review prudently the good faith estimate of closing costs (in your initial lender/broker RESPA signing meeting) which should include all fees being charged. Ask about each fee that you don't understand, and try to negotiate down the ones that seem excessive. Don't be afraid to ask questions about fees you don't understand!

9. Make sure you *plan for closing costs.* They are separate from your down payment money. At closing day, when you are scheduled to get your loan and close on the house, you will be expected to write a check for a number of expenses, which were outlined earlier in this chapter. Be aware that the closing costs can range somewhere between 1% to 3% of the selling price of the home. Plan for the closing costs by getting the good-faith estimate from your lender early in the loan process for pre-approval. Make sure you have the cash in your checking account and that it doesn't "disappear" before closing because of careless bookkeeping or a last minute emergency.

10. Have some *"extra cash" on hand after you purchase your home* and move in. Many people scrape and save all their money to pay for closing costs and down payment and leave little in the bank to cover any unforeseen circumstances that might arise. It costs money just to move in to your first home, plus all of the added expenses of owning your first home. You now need a lawnmower, washer and dryer, more furniture, among other items. Sometimes it can be overwhelming. Just plan to have some extra money in the bank to cover any emergencies, as well as money to make the first house payment. Some lenders require you to have three month's reserves after closing. It's a smart idea to have three month's reserves, which means a fund equal to three month's worth of expenses. This will help handle unexpected costs for home owner-ship and cover for stress levels you never thought you would see.

Be Aware of Amortization Schedules – Make them Work for You

My last bit of advice is to share with you, in the simplest way possible, how to amortize your home. To *amortize* from Webster's Dictionary is "to pay off a debt usually by periodic payments." A house payment is made up of two parts; the principal and the interest. The principal is the money that actually goes toward paying off the house while the interest is the part which goes to the banker; it's where they make their money on selling you the loan. One way to pay off your house quicker is to make extra principal payments. Remember you **HAVE** to keep making a house payment every month. The key here is to look at your amortization schedule (you require the lender to give you one at closing) and study it carefully. The schedule below is for a $100,000 loan, amortized or paid off over 30 years @ 6.5% interest with a level monthly payment of $632.07.

Payment Date Due	Mo. Payment	Principal Pd	Interest Pd	Balance
1. 08/01/04	632.07	90.40	541.67	99,909.60
2. 09/01/04	632.07	90.89	541.18	99,818.71
3. 10/01/04	632.07	91.39	540.68	99,727.32
4. 11/01/04	632.07	91.88	540.19	99,635.44
5. 12/01/04	632.07	92.38	539.69	99,543.06
Sub Total	**3,160.35**	**456.94**	**2,703.41**	
180 07/01/19	632.07	237.76	394.31	72,558.52
360 07/01/34	629.85	626.46	3.39	0.00
TOTAL	227,542.98	100,000.00	127,542.98	

As you can see on a $100,000 loan you pay interest charges of $127,542.98, thus making the total amount paid to the bank $227,542.98. **OUCH**! In this simple amortization schedule the first month you pay $541.67 of interest (which goes to the bank, this is how they make money) and only $90.40 is applied in principal to reduce the amount of money you owe on the loan.

One way to pay off your loan early is to make extra principal payments. I recommend you write a second check when you make extra principal payments (mark "early principal payment" in the lower left memo line of check) and make 1-2 extra payments as you can afford each month. As you can see by my chart above, extra principal payments would start out around $90.89 and gradually increase over the months ahead. Any early principal payments are direct reductions on the remaining principal on your loan. You must keep making your normal monthly $632.07 payment each month but if you keep up a steady discipline of making an extra principal payment each month it will save you a lot of interest you pay to the bank. After months of making extra principal payments (I check them off with a red ink pen on my amortization printout) call the lender and see where the balance on your loan stands. After a couple of years, if you decide to stay in the house and have made steady "extra principal" payments, look at refinancing the lower loan amount, maybe even to a 20 or 15 year fixed loan. Then start all over again making early principal payments to the new "refinanced" loan.

Acknowledgments for this Chapter include:

U.S. Department of Housing and Urban Development.
Alternative Mortgage Solutions, Crestwood, Missouri.

Recommended web site:

Becoming a Home Owner (fanniemae.com).

Recommended books include:

Essential Guide to Real Estate Contracts, by Mark Warda, Sphinx Publishing.
The Everything Homebuying Book, by Mark Weiss and Ruth Rejnis, Adams Media Corporation.
Tips & Traps for New Home Owners, by Robert Irvin, McGraw Hill.

NOTES:

_____

_____

_____

_____

_____

_____

_____

_____

_____

_____

_____

_____

_____

_____

_____

_____

_____

_____

_____

_____

_____

_____

_____

_____

_____

NOTES:

_____

_____

_____

_____

_____

_____

_____

_____

_____

_____

_____

_____

_____

_____

_____

_____

_____

_____

_____

_____

_____

_____

_____

_____

_____

6

FINANCIAL PLANNING

Opening Statement: I am not a Financial Planner or a Certified Financial Planner. All the information that I am sharing with you in this chapter is based upon research and the very fundamentals of what I believe you should know for financial planning. Financial programs such as stocks & bonds, mutual funds, 401K programs, SEP Plans, and more, can change. There are guidelines, regulations, and standards in the financial arena that I want you to look at carefully after you read and study this chapter. I recommend highly that you talk to the Professionals: a Financial Planner, Life Insurance Agent, Car/Auto Insurance agents who are state licensed and make their living in the financial and insurance industry.

Getting Started

Start investing young and start **NOW**! Don't depend upon anyone but yourself. The earlier you start investing the better return on your money you will see down the road for retirement. I will use this cliché a lot: "People don't plan to fail...they just fail to plan." As we will learn later on in this chapter, time, rate of return and compounding interest are your friends. Be wise and read this chapter over a couple of times to let financial planning sink in.

If you can manage this simple early investment, I encourage you to set your planning for future finances as soon as you graduate High School. Take the money you receive from your graduation party and invest lump sum money into a mutual fund. Set a goal at $500 or

$1000 and invest that money into a savings vehicle. By starting young, you will have made a key principle of allowing time and compounding interest work for you. Later in the chapter we will focus on this initial investment you have just started.

A Look at My Measurement Methods

The first measurement goal I want to share with you is my **10x10x80 Measurement Method**. This is a basic concept that has been around for a while. My father first shared this similar concept with me when I graduated high school. The theory behind this method is to give 10%, save 10% and live on 80%.

Giving 10% of your money off the top of what you earn will pay dividends in many areas. Look at giving 10% to your local church you attend; if you don't attend a church look at giving to different charities: Shriner's Hospital, World Missions, Feed the Hungry, etc. There are many ways to be a giver of your money. It does help as a tax deduction and with the taxes we pay this is a benefit. On top of this, being a giver and helping other people will make you a better person. Giving will come back to help you in other areas. Just don't overlook the positive method of giving 10%.

Saving 10% of your money will help you in the driver's seat. You start to take control of your finances when you save. Saving money is just the opposite of how many Americans today are living. Society teaches us to spend money, buy new and buy it now! And of course buy it on credit. Put it on charge and pay it off later, right? Wrong! Borrowing money costs in interest and it can be expensive. Think about this example:

If you save money at 10% interest and are not borrowing money at 10% interest, your are gaining a 20% interest benefit. Saving money, having it earn interest and watching it compound is a wise decision. (We'll learn more about compounding interest later). The other advantage of saving money is the "peace of mind" it generates. Just knowing you have money set aside to help you when bombshells hit the home turf. You lose your job, the car needs a new transmission, the roof leaks, your mate has a serious illness...and that financial crisis hits very hard. But...if you are a **SAVER**, you have a cushion.

Living on 80% of what you bring home is not impossible. You can do it if you start out working the 10x10x80 rule right away. It might be challenging at first, but if you discipline yourself and learn to live this formula, down the road you will see incredible growth in your life. Financial planning or lack of it can cause some serious problems. I have experienced debt and financial strains. Physically it can wear you down, and mentally – emotionally drain. Work at all costs to save, stay out of debt, and pay the bills you have in a monthly, timely manner.

The other method you can choose is the **0x10x90 Measurement Method.** I don't recommend this because of my strong belief in giving. With this approach you give 0%, you save 10% and live on 90%. The numbers change a little but you make the decision, which plan best works for you. You might see a better fit for your plans to start out with a **10x5x85 Measurement Method**. Give 10%, save 5% and live on 85%. Whatever plan fits your individual commitments and desires, choose one and be faithful to that plan!

The most important goal in financial planning is learning to take control of your personal situation. How do we build security in an uncertain world? The solution is you **HAVE** to take control and build financial security for yourself and your family. Work extremely hard to take charge of your money; your spending habits, your budget planning, your job income, and every facet of your financial life. From your earliest days you have been dependent upon your parents. Later on as you gain independence you rely on your bank for a checking account/savings program, then the lender to buy a home or a car. Many of these institutions offer products and programs for which we decide what will suit our needs. My premise is that "lack of control" means dependence on others, where as independence puts you more "in control." Think about it...you *can control* your plans for retirement, ways to reduce taxes, generate income diversification, and maximize your investment potential. Hopefully this chapter will help with your future financial planning.

We learn a lot in High School and College, but we aren't taught the basic principles of how money works. Financial planning 101 is a course we take for granted. Financial mistakes we make down the road of life can costs us dearly. The average person devotes hundreds of hours to their jobs each year but spend a fraction of that time on their financial planning. Most people will invest hours to look at magazines, surf the web, talk to dealers to buy a car, purchase a new stereo, and buy an appliance or a new computer. They will probably spend more time planning their summer vacation then they do on planning their future. You have two choices. You can do nothing, and let your "financial future" takes it course. Most people who follow this method end up broke, busted or disgusted. Or, you can begin learning about money, spend some time understanding the principles of building security, managing your assets along with your debts, and protecting your wealth as it increases. Choose the pain of discipline **NOW** or suffer the pain of **REGRET** later. Don't be a procrastinator; make the correct choice early while you are young!

Call Upon the Experts

My best advice is to seek a reputable financial planner or finance person. Ask your parents, friends and co-workers for referrals. I found there is a Financial Planning Association (FPA). The FPA supports the Certified Financial Planner (CFP) designation. Members can obtain this designation by passing the requirements of the Certified Financial Planner Board of Standards Inc. To find a financial planner in your area you can search the FPA's National Financial Planning support center @ (fpanet.org).

A quick overview of a Financial Planning Analysis (FPA) might work like this. It will have two major components. The **profile** will include a series of questions concerning your basic financial and personal information. This information will be used throughout the analysis to help formulate your goals. The **proposal** will contain an accumulation of visual charts, graphs, and data to illustrate your current financial status and future financial goals. The **profile** is usually broken into about a dozen sections that could look like this:

1. Client and agent information
2. Current financial position
3. Rates of return and inflation assumptions
4. Current monthly cash flow
5. Breakdown of consumer debt
6. Mortgage acceleration-relating to your home mortgage program
7. Major purchases
8. College education
9. Retirement
10. Income Protection
11. Emergency Fund
12. Creation of a will

Your financial planner should cover the following information:
- Explain the services they will provide, and outline responsibilities on both your own and the planners part. At this point, a planner should quote a fee estimate for services rendered and a time frame for the plan.
- Work closely with you in gathering your personal and business information (your profile)
- Analyze and evaluate your financial status. Discussions with your financial planner might include: tax planning, cash-flow management, estate planning, risk management, retirement planning, investments, education needs, and wills.
- Create a specific plan and present recommendations, based upon an analysis of your financial situation.
- Implement these plans, as well as sometimes working together with other professional advisers, such as accountants, insurance agents and lawyers to complete the plan successfully.
- Monitor the entire plan over time, continue to revisit your changing needs (family additions, deaths, divorce) and evaluate its progress to make adjustments as necessary.

Quick Review on Budget

Here we are again talking about money and that always relates back to your budget. The budget is the foundation of all of our financial planning. I plan to just review the budget process with a quick 5-step planning guide.

Step 1 – "Money IN" or Monthly Income

-Salary	-Tips
-Part-time work	-Tax Refunds
-Bonuses/commissions	-Dividends/Investments

Step 2 – Giving 10%

From your total monthly income you will determine your giving, based upon 10% of your gross monthly income. Write the first check to:

-Local Church	-Feed the Hungry Mission
-Community Charities	-Shriner's Hospital
-Children's Cancer Society	-Other

Step 3 – Saving 10%

The next check you write goes to your future investment program. Once you achieve your investment goals, pay that amount into those accounts:

-Life Insurance   -401 (k) program
-Savings Account   -Stocks/bonds
-Mutual Funds   -Rental property

Step 4 – Monthly Fixed Expenses

These are steady monthly payments, you have little control over them but they are very important, keep them current and make changes as necessary.

-Rent/House mortgage   -Child care
-Electricity/heating   -Health insurance
-Auto loan   -Telephone/cell bill
-Credit cards   -Other

Step 5 – Variable Expenses

These expenses can vary depending upon how much money is remaining after the above steps have been expensed. Work diligently not to spend more then you have allotted in your budget. By keeping accurate records each month, you know what you are spending at all times.

-Food   -Medicine
-Clothing   -School loans
-Home repairs   -Personal care
-Auto repairs   -Gifts
-Gas for automobile   -Entertainment

Setting Goals

Remember to set short-term and long-term goals. Your financial planner will help you with some of the long-range financial goals but have ideas of your own, think about them at a young age. Your short-term goals are quickly realized and very specific in nature. Planning to buy a piece of new furniture, trading in your car for a newer model, saving money for a vacation. These goals require a short period of discipline and yet you will see immediate results for your effort and time spent.

Long-term goals for financial retirement, building your dream house or college education for your children require a lot more discipline and planning over a larger period of time. For your long-term financial goals, write them down and have a plan on how to get there. Seek professional financial planners to help you begin early in life. Once you have the first job and are receiving a solid monthly income – start right away to invest in yourself. One method I recommend is to open a ROTH IRA; you can start this savings program with as little as $25.00 per month. The other option is to enroll ASAP in your company 401 (k) program, contribute and start investing immediately!

Earning Money and Keeping Money

Your income is an important part of your daily life. It's the money you bring home to live on. So your income is important, but it's not what your earn – it's what you **KEEP** that counts. Money can be a solution instead of a problem. As you understand how money works and the basics of certain financial formulas and principles, you can start taking control of your money and making it work for you. Lets look at how much money you might earn over a period of 40 years. Most people begin working in their 20's and hope to retire in their 60's.

$20,000 a year X 40 years = $ 800,000
$30,000 a year X 40 years = $1,200,000
$40,000 a year X 40 years = $1,600,000
$50,000 a year X 40 years = $2,000,000
$60,000 a year X 40 years = $2,400,000
$70,000 a year X 40 years = $2,800,000
$80,000 a year X 40 years = $3,200,000

Hmm! If you make just $30,000 a year, over 40 years you'll earn over a million dollars! If you do well and make $60,000 a year, you'll earn $2.4 million. That's a lot of money that will pass through your checking account in your lifetime. If you are married and your spouse and you both work, wow...the figures can really get crazy. So, by this example you can see that you are capable of becoming wealthy. The money potential for over a million dollars worth is there. You agree?

Then why are so many people in America not able to retire at 62 to 65 or 70? Because they are still **working for their money** and haven't learned the principles of **making their money work for them**.

People don't "plan to fail"…they just "fail to plan"

The following is a list I have compiled from my internet research, reading and studying of why people fail with their financial planning. It is useful information so that you don't make some of the same mistakes.

1. **Lack of understanding of how money works.** Most people don't invest the time or effort to learn how to manage their money. Taking a college class on money management is a step in the right direction as well as seeking professional advice from a financial consultant.

2. **No financial goals or written plan.** Many people are not goal setters, and they "brush off" financial planning until it is usually too late in life to start saving. My own personal opinion is people can be lazy in looking hard and strong at their specific, individual financial long term planning needs. Americans haven't been taught in school to deal with a budget, how money works, or the importance of saving for retirement.

3. **They don't think they have the "smarts" or the knowledge.** Many people think the rich know something they don't. They assume that financial wizards charge monster fees, offer techniques that aren't available to someone making $45,000 a year. **WRONG!** The same money management principles the wealthy use are available to everyone. The only difference is you may not have the extra money to take higher risks, which can equate to higher returns. A lot of money is lost and gained by investments. I will discuss this later in the chapter.

4. **Lack of time spent on learning about money.** A lot of people don't take the "quality" time they need to invest in their future. Our lives are so hectic, and fast-paced, with trying to balance a job, raise a family, work out at the gym and keep a social calendar, etc... They can't afford to take a couple hours during the week and spend time with a consultant on a weekend to mess with financial planning. **WRONG!** They can't afford not to!

5. **They don't think they have enough money.** Most people end up with more month then money. If you don't have any money left at the end of the month, how can you save money? Work your budget carefully and diligently, pack a sack lunch, take the Metro a couple days a week, cut your own hair, put off buying

new clothes. Somewhere...somehow...some way you can free up the money, no matter how tight it seems – just **DO IT**! **Note:** Knowing what I have learned now, if I had this guide back in my early twenties, I would have taken on an extra job or two during a month to make an my extra $100 a month to invest in my future.

6. **Procrastination**. Nothing happens until you set up a plan and "take action" to act upon it. This is one area where my wife and I plead guilty. In our early years of marriage we just kept putting off a solid financial plan for our future. The most important decision you can make is to start investing early in life and stay disciplined to save money for retirement, no matter what gets in your way.

7. **Impact of Inflation**. Whether you realize it or not, the cost of living seems to increase yearly. When I was a grade school kid in the sixties, I remember helping my dad pump gas at the station, a gallon of gas was twenty cents a gallon; move ahead to 2005 and today a gallon of gas is two dollars and twenty cents. My 3 speed Huffy bicycle which I wanted for my 10 year birthday was twenty-six dollars plus tax, that same bike today would cost easy around a hundred dollars. How will the dollars you save for the future compare with the cost of living at retirement age? It is something to think about, and consulting with a financial planner to help you overcome the deficit is another key to investing.

Keys to Implementing Wealth

Planning is the first step in taking control of your financial freedom. We all have plans to build financial security for our families, but in reality many people do nothing or at the very least contribute very little to reach their financial goals. As I have stated earlier, most people have more days left then money at the end of the month. One solution can be to reposition your income and your assets and live on less money. What are some ways to help you keep your priorities straight? What are some avenues to separate your "wants" from your "needs"? Take a look at the following guidelines I recommend:

- Pay yourself first (Be one of the top five first bills you pay each month).
- Adjust your priorities, make changes periodically.
- Establish a budget (This is a key element to financial foundation).
- Adjust your lifestyle, make some critical changes, and distinguish between what you want and what you need.

- Avoid the credit card trap. Pay off those charges at the end of each billing period. Watch out for those installment loans (no interest fees for 12 months – they suck you in); save money and pay cash.
- Earn additional income to invest young, take on a second job on the weekends.
- As soon as you can, start a savings plan by investing in a mutual fund, an IRA or your companies 401 (k) program.

There are many ways to build financial freedom and build your wealth for your future. Money management programs abound in magazines, books, financial literature and on the Internet, but I want to just take a look at six simple key principles that can help you have a better understanding of how you can have money work for you, not against you. If you were to take the time to study and research on your own, I am sure you would come across these six money principles. They are:

#1 The "Pay Yourself First" Principle

The first step toward building financial security is paying yourself first. I revert back to my two measurement plans, the 10x10x80 or the 0x10x90 methods. Choose either one, but the first step is to put yourself at the top of the list. That means putting yourself, your family, your future, ahead of the mortgage, utilities, food, and all the other requirements on your money. Before anyone else stakes a claim to your money, pay yourself by putting a specific amount aside in an investment account or a savings plan.

The standard goal would be 10% of your income. If you can't possibly budget that target make it at least 5% and set a goal to build up to 10% savings of your monthly income. By following this principle you are at least heading in the right direction. To manage a savings program start out building two types of basic accounts:

Emergency fund – Take 5% of your savings each month and put that money into an emergency cash reserve fund. This fund should be built up to cover at least 3-6 months of income for unexpected expenses such as loss of a job, serious illness, automobile problems, or major household repairs. By having an emergency fund in place you have peace of mind, protection against financial disaster, or being forced to take money from your long-range savings plan. Once you have a sufficient emergency fund established, apply that 5% money toward your long-term savings vehicle. Two key points to apply here:

1. **Put money in the emergency fund and leave it there.** Don't treat the emergency fund like a checking account where you "put and take." It is a savings account for emergencies! Things like vacation money, anniversary weekends, and luxury items should be part of the budget process and funded through your income after savings.

2. **Invest money for your emergency reserve in a money market vehicle.** They tend to have a competitive rate of return, easy access to your money, with usually a $1000.00 minimum balance required and often times offer check-writing capabilities.

Long Range Savings or Investment Plan – This is your long-term account designed for retirement savings, college education for your children, and any other long range investment goals you desire. Here is where a CFP can assist you in making the right decisions that fit your future plans. Seek professional guidance! There are a variety of long-range investment programs, which I will discuss later in the chapter. Here it is wiser to "invest" your money for the long haul rather then "save" money in an investment account. After meeting and discussing your unique program with a professional finance person, definitely plan to use direct deposit from your checking account. I find it's too hard to have money in the checking account and not spend it. The temptation to use that money somewhere else is too irresistible. Simply arrange with your bank or employer to have a set amount of money each month deposited directly into your investment vehicles each month. That way the money goes into that account before you even see it on your check. The beauty of direct deposit is it forces you to "save money" vs. "spend money."

#2 The Principle of "Time"

Our time is one of the most valued possessions we have. What we do with our time, as the years move along, really can have a huge impact on financial planning for the future. Today, many people are living longer with better health and exercise habits. If you take that amount of time start investing **EARLY** in life it will yield large financial success stories for you. Time is really an underrated tool for many people in the financial game. They don't understand that time, in combination with consistency and rate of return, is a powerful principle to achieving financial security.

TIME + Rate of Return + CONSISTENCY = <u>FINANCIAL SECURITY</u>

Study the example below to grasp this concept. Let's say some parent's deposit $1000 in a simple investment program for their child that earns a 7% rate of return. If you don't add any more money, and don't touch that account by age 65, that $1000 would escalate to $81,272. Parents make a one time $1000 investment at a 7% rate of return:

> At birth to age 65, this would total $81,272.
> Start at age 16 to age 65, this would total $27,529.
> Start at age 40 to age 65, this would total $5,427.

See what the power of time can do for you!

One of the biggest financial mistakes people make is assuming they don't have extra money to save. Once you have a job, you have income and you have money somewhere to put aside and start saving. The sooner you begin the wiser investor you become. Talk to a financial expert about putting money in a Mutual Fund account when you get your first job. My research shows you can put as little as $25 a month in this savings vehicle. Even if you have to start with a smaller monthly investment, the important key is to begin immediately and add more money as your budget can permit. See my examples of monthly investments and what they can yield over a 40 year time period.

> $25 a month for 40 years @ 10% rate of return = $132,777.
> $50 a month for 40 years @ 10% rate of return = $265,555.
> $75 a month for 40 years @ 10% rate of return = $398,333.
> $100 a month for 40 years @ 10% rate of return =$531,111.

The example shows the difference between saving $25 a month and stretching your savings to $100 a month. It might be very advantageous when you're young to get a second job one to two weekends a month to clear $100 and dedicate that money to a savings program. I know now that when I was in my mid twenties and not married...I should have pushed the pedal a little harder. I could have waited tables or detailed cars on a weekend to make that extra $100 cash to put into a savings plan for my future.

Here is an example of saving $100 a month/$1200 a year @ 8% rate of return to age 60 would yield:

Starting at age 20 in 40 years the total would be $310,868.
Starting at age 30 in 30 years the total would be $135,940.
Starting at age 35 in 25 years the total would be $ 87,777.
Starting at age 40 in 20 years the total would be $ 54,914.

The importance of making **TIME** work to your advantage can't be overstated. You can either make time the critical component of your plan or you can wait and make money the most important factor. Remember, the longer you wait the more money you need to add the later in life you start investing. (You play catch up). If you are like most young people you don't have a lot of extra money and that's why time is so critical to your future. Invest small amounts early vs. waiting to save and have to save larger amounts later in life. Time can be your worst enemy or your best friend. Start investing **YOUNG** and make **TIME** your friend. The other pal (friend/co-worker) you need is **CONSISTENCY**. Be faithful, fixed, firm, and dedicated to making those small monthly investments, because consistency is the fuel that will make your investments excel!

#3 The "Rate of Return" Principle

The rate of return is usually related to the interest rate your investment provides over a period of time, generally in years. By investing money in a money market your rate of return will be about 2-5% depending upon the market. It is a safe investment and you will not lose money. The greater the risk the bigger the reward. Investors with money to burn might invest in foreign funds that could bear a rate of return of 12-18% but they could also take a dive and plummet to 5%.

The difference between a percent or more can make a difference. The impact of the rate of return, combined with **TIME**, can be substantial. You might think that if you earned 10% rate of return versus a 5% rate of return your money would double. **WRONG**! Because of the power of compound interest that 5% difference adds up to a lot more money over time, then you realize. See my example below:

$100/month @ 5% rate of return over 40 years   = $148,856.
$100/month @ 10% rate of return over 40 years = $559,461.

TIME + Rate of Return + CONSISTENCY = MAXIMUM GROWTH

Remember, the higher the rate the harder your investments are working for you, but also keep in mind the greater the risk the greater the loss can be.

How to calculate the Rate of Return: $(N-Y)/T = Rate of Return$

N = Value of your investment.

Y = Value of your investment when you bought it.

T = Time you held the investment. (T is always calculated in years; if you hold an investment for 15 years and 3 months T = 15.25 years).

#4 The Principle of "Compounding Interest"

I used to think that the interest rate on an investment was pretty simple. You invest your money at 5% and get "X" amount. Then if your investment returned 10%, it would be two times "X" right? **WRONG!** Then someone sat me down and shared with me a "compound interest" table and explained the magic of compound interest.

Remember the example of the parents who deposited $1000 at 7% interest at their child's birth to celebrate? If we figure 7% interest a year, the annual interest would be $70. And $70 a year multiplied by 65 years equals $4,550. Then how did we end up with a figure of $81,272 at age 65? Ahh. The magic and power of compounding interest. Let's see how it really works:

The first year of the deposit, @ 7% = $70, which is credited to the $1,000 to make $1,070. When the interest is credited the following year, the 7% interest rate is calculated on $1,070, not $1,000. So the new interest amount credited is now $74.20, making the total at the end of the second year $1,144. As the account grows, each year the interest payment is calculated on the total in the account, including all the past interest payments. Compounding the interest is how $1,000 grew to $81,272 over 65 years. So with the power of compounding interest at work, your money goes from a couple hundred dollars to a thousand plus very quickly.

#5 The "Rule of 72" Principle

A simple concept called the Rule of 72 can show the exciting impact of time and compounding. The Rule of 72 says that your money will approximately **DOUBLE** at a point in time, determined by dividing 72 by the percent interest you earn. The Rule of 72 shows the astounding way your money can compound if you just give it enough time.

Your money will double in:

72 divided by 2% interest = 36 years.
72 divided by 4% interest = 18 years.
72 divided by 6% interest = 12 years.
72 divided by 8% interest = 9 years.
72 divided by 10% interest = 7.2 years.
72 divided by 12% interest = 6 years.

Let's look at an example of "waiting to invest your money." Remember that starting younger pays bigger dividends over the long run. If you save $50 a month at 10% interest and start this program at age 25, see how it can cost you the longer you wait.

Begin Saving at:	Total at Age 65	Cost to Wait
Age 25	$265,555	
Age 30	$162,614	$102,941
Age 35	$ 98,696	$166,859
Age 40	$ 59,008	$206,547
Age 45	$ 34,364	$231,191
Age 50	$ 19,063	$246,492

#6 The "Diversification" Principle

It's especially important to diversify your equity investments. Owning and investing your money into different types of vehicles such as CD's, stocks, bonds, and real estate can be a key to growing a diversified retirement portfolio. Over time long-term stocks and mutual funds can be a solid plan. Take the time to research for yourself to gain a better perspective. In my in depth study, you should diversify in income, growth, growth and income programs, some international growth stocks, as well as mutual funds that do business globally. Investing in mutual funds is a great way to spread your risk because mutual funds buy capital in a number of different stocks so a decline in an individual stock can be cushioned by an upswing in another. When looking at the bond market you have a slower, steady balance, thus you will reduce your interest rate risk. A good mix of corporate bonds, bond funds and some government bonds will help balance the rise and fall of interest rates. Diversification also helps you hedge against loss while providing safety and flexibility. Here is an example of a diversified game plan:

$^1/_3$ of your retirement from Social Security benefits.

$^1/_3$ of your retirement from your Employers Plan (pensions, 401 (k), profit-sharing, SEP).

$^1/_3$ of your retirement from your personal savings program (investments in mutual funds, IRA's, stocks, bonds, rental properties).

Understanding Asset Allocation

Asset allocation is a method of combining asset classes such as bonds, stocks, and cash in an investment portfolio in order to meet your financial goals. The asset allocation decision is an important key factor in determining both the risk and the return of an investment portfolio. An asset is defined as anything that can be bought and sold, that produces income, such as stocks and bonds or CDs. Asset classes can be grouped together with similar goals, properties, and characteristics. An example of asset grouping would be government bonds, large corporate stocks, and money-market mutual funds.

Factors that can influence the asset allocation decision would include your financial needs and goals, your attitude toward risk, and the time frame of your investment planning.

An Overview of Social Security Benefits

Social Security pays retirement, disability, family and survivors benefits. The Social Security administration office has a toll free number to call to understand more about your own personal retirement benefits. Call and ask for your Earnings and Benefit Statement. The number is 800-772-1213. They will send you a form asking how much you earned last year, your estimated earnings for this year, the age you plan to retire and your estimated annual earnings. Here are some things to be aware of:

1.   Make sure you have an idea of your social security benefit, get an idea of what your benefits are now and what they are forecasted to be when you retire.
2.   Verify your social security record every 2-3 years.
3.   Keep in mind that if you delay your retirement you'll increase your social security benefits.

Retirement – If you were born before 1938, your full retirement age is 65. Because of a 1983 law change, the full retirement age will increase gradually to 67 for people born in 1960 or later. You can retire as early as 62 and take your benefits at a reduced rate. If you continue working after your full retirement age, you can receive higher benefits because of additional earnings and special credits for delayed retirement.

Disability – If you become disabled before full retirement age, you can receive disability benefits after six months if you have: A) enough credits from earnings (depending on your age, you must have earned 6-20 of your credits in 3-10 years before you became disabled); and B) a physical or mental impairment that's expected to prevent you from doing "substantial" work for a year or more or may result in death. Note: In talking to my financial consultant I discovered that disability is very hard to qualify for, 70% of entries get turned down.

Family – If you're eligible for disability or retirement benefits, your current or divorced spouse, minor children or adult children disabled before age 22 also may receive benefits. Each may qualify for up to about 50% of your benefit amount. The total amount depends on how many family members qualify.

Survivors – When you die, certain members of your family may be eligible for benefits:

- Your spouse age 60 or older (50 or older if disabled, or any age if caring for your children younger that age 16) and
- Your children if unmarried and younger than age 18, still in school and younger than age 19, or adult children disabled before age 22.

If you are divorced, your ex-spouse could be eligible for a widow's or widower's benefit on your record when you die.

For further information, their web site is (socialsecurity.gov)

Source: Social Security Form SSA-7005-SM-S1 (01-2004)

Be Aware of Inflation

Inflation is a component you must consider in your financial planning goals. The rate of inflation has a specific impact on your buying power. Nearly every area of your financial game plan is affected, from your job income, your investments, to your personal savings. Inflation is defined as a process on continuously rising prices, or equivalently of a continuously falling value of money. Being aware of inflation helps you be a better investor. An example, if you earn a 4% rate of return on your savings or investment plan, and inflation is 5% you are losing money. For your investments to grow you must achieve a higher rate of return than the current inflation rate. Terms to understand are:

Consumer Price Index (CPI) – Measures inflation as experienced by consumers in their day-to-day living expenses. (It is sometimes referred to as the retail price index).

Producer Price Indexes (PPIs) – These are a family of indexes that measure the changes in the selling prices received by domestic producers of goods and services. They formerly were referred to as Wholesale Price Indexes. When the PPIs are released, the news media will most often report the percentage change in the index for Finished Goods.

Overview of Investment Retirement Plans and Programs

When you have a job you have to pay taxes. The more money you make the more taxes you pay. One way to help minimize your taxes is to look at tax shelters. By investing your money into IRA's, 401 (k)s, profit sharing, and SEP plans you can get a tax deferral. Understand that a deduction is an amount of money you can subtract from your gross income before you calculate taxes. The more you can reduce your gross income with deductions, (such as if you work from home, you can deduct your home office, a portion of the telephone bill, electricity, fax machine and copier and so on) the less the amount you'll pay on income taxes. It is to your advantage to deduct when/where you can. A deferral means that you can postpone (put off) payment of current taxes until a later date in the future. The advantage of deferring taxes is the likelihood that you will be in a lower tax bracket when you draw the money out and have to pay taxes on it. IRA's and 401 (k)s are tax-deferred plans, thus giving you a great tax shelter if you invest in them.

Traditional IRA

The Economic Recovery Tax Act of 1981 (ERAT) provided individuals the opportunity to prepare for their retirements through establishment of Individual Retirement Accounts. They can be funded in many ways, including CD's and passbook savings accounts, mutual funds, common stocks, bonds, investment trusts, and individual retirement annuities (fixed or variable). IRA's offer short-term tax savings by allowing you and your spouse the potential to invest $4,000 each off the top of your gross income, therefore reducing your taxable income. (If you are in a 35% tax bracket, you could save $700 in taxes in one year, just by opening an IRA). Earnings on your IRA are tax-deferred until retirement, when you will most likely be rated in a lower tax bracket. Generally, you cannot withdraw the money until at least age 59½ without a penalty. Withdrawing the money before this age will result in a 10% penalty, but, you must start to withdraw the money by age 70½.

Roth IRA

The Taxpayers Act of 1997 provided new options for taxpayers who want to save and invest money in a tax-deferred account. Some of the differences and advantages include:

*   No taxes will be owed on any distributions after age 59½ with certain conditions.
*   No contribution can be tax deductible.
*   Specific adjusted gross income limits determine eligibility for a Roth IRA.
*   There are no required distributions (as with a traditional IRA-must start by 70½), thus it allows for your money to grow tax-deferred for a longer period of time.
*   If beneficiaries inherit these accounts, they will owe no taxes on distributions.

401 (k) Plans

These plans work with guiding the retirement planning target away from the employer to the employee, instead of a guaranteed pension plan. The pension plan was based on salary and length of years with the company. Most larger corporations are moving away from the pension plan and offering their employees to contribute a certain percent of their salary up to a specified maximum amount. In a 401 (k) the employee contributes pretax money in specific investments and the employer often matches this contribution. 401 (k) plans are all set up differently, but in most cases the choices in these plans are specific mutual funds that are part of several fund families. Many times the family will include stock and bond funds, along with a money market fund. Typically, but not in every case, the employer will match their employees contributions. The combination of matching contributions and tax-deferred growth makes the 401 (k) plans one of the best investment vehicles. Check with your company's benefit department to see if your company provides a 401 (k) plan and if they do, invest the maximum allowed! **Note:** Try to interview with companies that offer 401 (k) plans, and after the waiting period, as soon as you can start with the program, jump at this opportunity. You cannot withdraw money before age 59½ and do not have to make withdrawals until age 70½. You can borrow money from your 401 (k), but I strongly urge you not to borrow unless an extreme emergency arises.

403 (b) Plans
Non-Profit companies and Public Schools have this program for their employees, which is very similar to the 401 (k) plan.

SEP Plans
There are three plans for self-employed people; they include SEP-IRA, SIMPLE plans, and Keogh plans. All three plans are tax deductible (unlike regular IRA's for many people). They grow tax-deferred like all other qualified retirement plans. They are subject to same age 70½ related distribution restrictions as traditional IRA's.

SEP-IRA – You, as the owner can set up to 15% of your income in an IRA, up to $25,500 now in 2005. Your business must contribute the same percentage that you set aside for yourself to employees who meet the following three guidelines and who elect to participate in the plan.

1.   They are at least 21 years of age.
2.   They earned at least $400 a year from the business.
3.   They have worked for this business for three of the last five years (including partial years).

SIMPLE – This plan was enacted by Congress in 1996, and is similar to a 401 (k) plan. Employers, including the owner, can set aside up to $10,000 of gross income into a SIMPLE if they meet two criteria:

1.   They earned at least $5,000 a year from this business.
2.   They have worked for this business for at least part of the last two years.

The business would contribute money for employees who elect to participate in the plan based upon the following two guidelines:

1.   For at least 3 of the next 5 years the matching amount is 3%, whereas in the other 2 years it can be less then 3%.

2. Every year, the matching contribution is 2%.

KEOGH – Keogh plans are also for the self-employed and their employees, and like SEP plans have similar advantages to IRAs. The main difference between a Keogh and a SEP-IRA is the contribution limit and paperwork requirements. Depending upon the type of Keogh plan selected, the participant can contribute much more money to this plan than to a SEP-IRA. There are three types of Keogh plans:

1. **Profit Sharing Keogh** – This plan has a 15% of the total payroll of the plan participants, including a compensation limit of $50,000 and a contribution limit of $25,500.

2. **Money Purchase Keogh** – This plan allows contributions from 1% to 25% of compensation, for 2005 the contributions are capped at $30,000. Once the % has been set, it cannot be changed for life of the plan. Contributions are mandatory for every year the plan is in existence.

3. **Paired Keogh** – This is a combination of the two plans, which allows more flexibility. Annual contributions are limited to 25% but can be as low as 3%. The amount contributed to the money purchase part is fixed for life of plan, but the amount contributed to the profit-sharing part (still subject to 15% limit) can change.

Corporate Pension Plans

As an incentive to remain with the company, some corporations offer retirement benefits to their employees. These retirement benefits are provided via a pension plan, an entity that is separate and distinct from the corporation. The qualified pension plan must have a vesting schedule, and the benefits of the plan must be available only to employees of the corporation and/or their beneficiaries. Unlike profit sharing plans, contributions are required even during unprofitable years. Pension plans are set up under a defined contribution plan or a defined benefit plan. If the corporation you work for offers pension plans contact the HR benefits department to find out their specific plan.

Profit-Sharing Plans

Some corporate companies and smaller business companies may offer profit-sharing plans. These are designed to allow the employees of a company to share in the profits they help create. In a profit-sharing plan, the employer contributes a percentage of its annual profits to a trust fund for the benefit of employees. The amount contributed may be at the discretion of the board of directors, the owner of the small business or it may be determined by a formula. If the company has a year where it doesn't make a profit, then no money is put into the employee's investment trust fund.

Annuities

Annuities are insurance contracts that work like a traditional IRA. Contributions are not tax deductible and taxes on the earnings are deferred until the money is withdrawn. Annuities stop paying upon death, whereas life insurance pays upon death of an individual. Annuities have often been nicknamed "upside down insurance." Annuities are generally purchased in order to provide a lifetime of income to an individual. Basically, the way annuities work is a certain amount of capital is invested with an insurance company, which in return promises to make certain payments to specific individuals upon tailored guidelines. Money is usually not withdrawn until age 59½ but annuity withdrawals do not have to begin at age 70½ and there is no limit on how much money you can put into an annuity. There are three types of annuities:

1. **Fixed Annuity** – The insurance company contracts to make fixed dollar payments to the annuitant for the term of the contract. The term of the contract is often the duration of the annuitant's life. They let you lock in a guaranteed rate of interest that will be earned on the invested capital. One key problem with a fixed annuity is that it does not allow for a hedge against inflation.

2. **Variable Annuity** – The insurance company contracts to make payments, which vary in amount. The term of the contract is for a specified period of time, generally the duration of the annuitant's life. The variable annuity gives you a choice of mutual fund like investments called sub-accounts. So your return depends on the performance of the particular funds. You can switch between mutual funds in the annuity without worrying about capital gains taxes. You can also switch the money from one annuity custodian to another. This annuity also gives you a number of withdrawal options, including guaranteed payments for the rest of your life.

3. **Combined Annuities** – This annuity contract is part fixed annuity and part variable annuity. A certain percentage of the invested capital may be placed in a fixed annuity, with the remainder going to a variable annuity. The thinking here is that this combined contract contains less investment risk than the variable annuity, while providing greater potential returns than a fixed annuity. In a time of recession, the variable portion would provide you with a hedge against inflation, while the fixed portion would provide you with a hedge against deflation.

I suggest fully investing in an IRA or 401 (k) program before moving on to any annuity investment programs. Annuities tend to have higher fees (cost to run them-custodial charges) including mutual fund fees and insurance charges.

What is Risk vs. Reward?

Many investors are faced with a trade off, they wish to preserve the money they are investing, but also want that investment to make more money. As investors we each have our own unique tolerance for risk. Keep in mind that generally the investments yielding the highest returns also generate the greatest risks. Let's take a quick look at different kinds of investment risks:

Market Risk – This relates to the market value of a security in the future. Market prices fluctuate and are susceptible to economic and financial trends, supply and demand, and many other factors which cannot be precisely predicted.

Financial Risk – This pertains to the future viability of a company, the risk is the uncertainty concerning the corporation that issued the security. Most business ventures have inherent financial risk. The future stability of a company cannot be guaranteed or predicted, nor can the price of its stock be foretold.

Interest Rate Risk – Interest rates change all the time. We have no way of knowing what the interest rate will be the following year.

Liquidity Risk – This relates to the potential ability or inability to sell and collect proceeds for a specific investment. Some securities are more liquid than others, so you have to take this fact into consideration. How soon can you get your cash?

Inflation Risk – Inflation, or the purchasing power risk, concerns the uncertainty of the future purchasing power of invested dollars.

The risk is that the rate of inflation will erode the purchasing power of fixed payments over time. Thus the value of a dollar today may be considerably less in the future due to declines in purchasing power.

Management Risk – The stability and expertise leadership of a corporation's management has a direct bearing on the financial and market risk of the company. We have already seen corporate management fiascoes with Enron, Worldcom, and Adelphia to name a few.

Taxation Risk – Changes in the tax laws can affect the future viability and attractiveness of certain investments.

Economic Risk – This involves the uncertainty of the economic, political and social environment. For example, a significant economic downturn affects the business market.

High Risk to Low Risk Investing Overview

High Risk – Foreign Investments/Junk Bonds/Futures/Options/ Speculative Land Purchase/Collectibles.

Medium Risk – Corporate Bonds/Stocks & Bond Mutual Funds/ Mortgage Backed Securities/ Rental Real Estate.

Low Risk – Treasury Bonds/Short-term Bond Funds/Life Insurance Contracts/Annuities/Zero-Coupon Bonds/Utility Stocks/Bank CDs/ T-Bills/Money-Market Mutual Funds/Savings Accounts.

The Bond Market

Corporations issue debt securities to raise money as part of their capital structure. Bonds are a form of long term financing for a corporation, usually with a maturity date of five to thirty years. When you buy a bond, you're basically lending a sum of money (the principal) to the issuer for a fixed period of time (the return). In return for the loan, the issuer pays you interest, computed on a fixed rate called the coupon rate. Interest is generally paid monthly or quarterly. When the bond matures, you receive your original principal; no matter how much the price of the bond fluctuated since it was issued. A bond is kind of like an IOU issued by a company, government, or some other institution. In the case of a bond, the issuer has more time to repay its debt.

One rule to remember about investing in bonds is their movement. Bond prices move in the opposite direction of interest rates. When interest rates go up, bond prices go down and when interest rates go down, bond prices go up.

Bonds carry rating such as AAA (highest rating) to a D (default rating). Agencies that conduct bond ratings include Fitch, Standard & Poor's, and Moody's. Analysts from theses companies study the detailed financial information and along with years of experience, assign a rating to each bond issuer.

For an example let's say you buy a $10,000 bond from XYZ Corporation. You have lent XYZ $10,000 and XYZ agrees to pay back the $10,000 at the end of 10 years, it also agrees to pay you 6% or $600 each year for use of your money. Thus, you have a fixed income of $600 every year from the bond.

Bond Quotations

All bonds are quoted on the basis of price or yield. When quoted on the basis of price, the quote is understood as a percentage of the par (face) value. A quote of 92 does not simply mean $92, but instead is 92% of the par value. Therefore, a bond with a par value of $1,000 would, at 92, translate to $920.

Bond Yields

Along with understanding the quoted prices of bonds you should be aware of the yield the bond will return to the investor. Though a bond has only one interest rate, there are four ways to calculate the yield:

1. **Nominal Yield** – The nominal yield (also known as the coupon rate) is the annual interest the bond will return to the owner. A 7% nominal yield on a $1,000 bond, for example, will result in an annual payment of $70 to the owner.

2. **Current Yield** – A bond can actually generate a larger or smaller current return to the investor than its nominal yield. This yield adjusts the bond's nominal yield for the bond's current price to determine what percentage you would receive if you bought the bond at its current price. In the above example, if the bond dropped in price from 70 to 60 the bond's value would fall from $1,000 to $940. At that price the current yield would rise to 7.4%.

Current yield is calculated below:

$$\frac{\$70 \text{ (annual interest payment of the bond)}}{\$940 \text{ (current market price of the bond)}} = 7.4 \text{ \% Current Yield}$$

3. **Yield to Maturity** – This is a measure of the bond's value from the date of purchase to the date of maturity, taking into account both the nominal yield and long-term effect of the market price. For example the $1,000 7% bond bought for $940 provides a return in two ways: annual interest and a profit of $60 when the bond is redeemed at face value upon maturity.

4. **Yield to Call** – This is the yield up to the first potential date at which the issuer can call, or redeem, the bond. Usually, there are several years before the bond matures. The calculations are more complicated on the yield to maturity and yield to call, I suggest asking your broker to help you with these yields, depending upon the bond you are investing in.

Bonds can be a key investment vehicle in your financial planning. They allow you to lock in a specific rate of income for a long period of time, which helps build stability to your financial planning foundation. Later in the chapter we will take a look at high risk vs. low risk investment vehicles.

Types of Bonds

Corporate Bonds – These bonds are issued by corporations, yet unlike the government or municipalities, they may not always be around forever. Corporate bonds are issued in denominations of $1,000 (their par value) and pay the investor semi-annually.

Mortgage Bonds – First mortgage bonds are secured by a mortgage on all or a portion of any of the fixed property, equipment, or machinery. They are the safest and highest grade of corporate bonds because they provide an undisputed claim to fixed assets held by the corporation. First mortgage bonds indicate a priority on assets. Junior mortgage bonds have secondary claims on assets. There are two types of mortgage bonds:

General mortgage bonds and Consolidated mortgage bonds. In the event of liquidation, first mortgage bonds have priority and junior mortgage bonds are next in line.

Collateral Trust Bonds – These trust bonds are secured by the collateral of another corporation, usually in the form of debt and equity securities. The corporation issuing the bonds deposits stocks and bonds of another corporation (usually those of a subsidiary) with their trustee to secure the bond.

Municipal Bonds – These bonds are very popular for the simple fact that the interest they pay is totally free from federal taxes. They are issued by states, counties, cities, towns, villages and taxing authorities of many types, (in many cases bondholders who are residents of the states issuing the bonds don't have to pay state or local taxes on the interest). There are two main types of municipal bonds:

1. **General Obligation Bonds** – they are secured by the taxing authority of the municipal issuer and are backed by that entity's full faith and credit. General use bonds are used to fund school districts and other projects.

2. **Revenue Bonds** – These bonds are tax-exempt bonds issued for a specific purpose by a municipality. They are secured by the revenues, which will be generated by the project, such as toll roads, power plants, bridges, airports, hospitals as well as other projects.

Junk Bonds – These bonds can be very risky, sometimes called high-yield bonds, they are issued by corporations that have lower investment grade rating. They are companies that get a Better Business Bureau rating, and are either on their way up or on their way down in terms of their financial stability.

Foreign Bonds – These bonds are foreign government bonds backed by the full faith and credit of the issuing countries. While U.S. government treasuries are sound, you need to pay careful attention investing in foreign bonds. Industrialized countries like England, France and Germany will carry more weight than developing countries like Argentina or Kenya. Although the yields on foreign bonds can carry significantly higher returns and stronger capital gains, they are riskier. Depending upon the country you might have to invest at least $20,000 in one bond, for instance.

Agency Bonds – These bonds are issued by U.S. government agencies and carry an implied government guarantee. They rank one notch below actual U.S. government securities in terms of safety because they are not direct obligations of the U.S. government, as are government bonds. Agencies such as the Federal Land Banks and Federal Credit Banks issue debt to finance agricultural projects. There are agencies that issue debt securities to finance housing and mortgage projects. In most cases it is understood that in the unlikely event that any of the agencies would default on their debt service, the federal government would step in and guarantee payment.

Convertible Bonds – These bonds are a mix, where one part is a bond and one part is a stock. As bonds, they offer regular fixed income though usually at a yield lower than straight bonds that a corporation might issue. On the stock side, convertibles can offer strong potential for appreciation, especially from the issuing company's financial success. They can offer high income and appreciation potential yet also offer lower income than typical bonds and less appreciation than common stock offers.

U.S. Savings Bonds – Instead of a corporation, municipality or state bond, the federal government also issues savings bonds. They are the safest possible fixed income securities since they are backed by the full faith and credit of the U.S. government. They pay a fixed interest rate and have a specific maturity date. The interest paid is federally taxable, but not state taxable. You can purchase government bonds from your local bank, directly through the Federal Reserve Bank or for a fee from a brokerage firm. There are two series of U.S. Savings bonds, which are Series EE and HH.

1. **Series EE Bonds** – EE Bonds are appreciation bonds which are sold at deep discounts usually 50% of their face value. The difference between the purchase price and the face value at maturity represents the interest paid over the life of the savings bond. They have no set maturity date and pay no interest, but you can redeem them any time, after six months of buying them to as long as 30 years. You can start one for as little as $25; they are issued in denominations of $50, $75, $100, $200, $500, $1,000, $5,000 and $10,000.

2. **Series HH Bonds** – HH Bonds are current-income securities, which are bought at their face value and which receive semi-annual, interest payments. They carry maturity dates of ten years, and there is a penalty for early redemption. HH Bonds can only be redeemed at the Federal Reserve Bank. At issue... the interest rate reflects the current rate of interest, and once issued, the rate of interest never changes.

Treasury Bonds – These bonds are long-term bonds issued by the federal government with maturity dates from ten to thirty years. They typically yield less than corporate bonds because of their inherent safety, being backed by the government. They are most commonly in minimum increments of $1,000 but also $5,000, $10,000, $100,000 and $1,000,000 sizes. Yields on government bonds fluctuate on the secondary market and are influenced by prevailing interest rates. The semi-annual interest paid on government bonds is federally taxable but exempt from state tax.

U.S. Treasury Bills – T-Bills, as they are commonly known, are the most marketable of government securities. They are short-term obligations with maturity dates of 3 months, 6 months, or a year. They trade at a discount, meaning that an investor can purchase them for less than the face value of the bill. The difference between the discount and the face value is the interest earned on the Treasury bill. Interest earned is federally taxable, but exempt from state tax. The minimum investment for Treasury bills is $10,000. The main attraction for these bills is their safety, liquidity, and rate of return.

U.S. Treasury Notes – Treasury notes are fixed-income, interest-bearing securities issued by the U.S. government with maturity dates ranging from two to ten years. They pay a fixed rate of interest semi-annually, have a stated maturity date, and are actively traded in the secondary market. These notes are usually issued in $1,000 denominations.

Zero-Coupon Bonds – These bonds are also called zeros for short. They are issued with a 0 percent coupon rate. Instead of making regular interest payments to the investor, a zero-coupon bond is issued at a deep discount from its face value of $100 or $5,000. The return comes from the gradual income in the bond's price from the discount to face value, which it reaches at maturity. Two benefits occur with this slow but steady rise:

1. You know exactly how much money you will receive when the bond matures.
2. You know exactly the date when you will receive that money.

Because zeros have a specific schedule of appreciation, you should use a zero as a key part of investing for specific areas of your financial plan, such as a college education for your children. Seek professional advice when working with zero-coupon bonds.

Unit Investment Trusts – These UITs, as they are sometimes called, buy a fixed portfolio of bonds and hold them to their maturity dates. They contrast with bond funds, which continually buy and sell bonds and never mature. A UIT can be bought from a broker for a minimum of $1,000. You will usually pay a 5% sales charge to the broker up front upon purchase and then a 1-2% annual management expense fee thereafter. UITs offer a fixed monthly income check, you buy into a diverse portfolio of trusts, you know exactly what assets the trusts holds before you buy it and if you need access to your capital (money) you can sell your units back to the broker, but you might have to sell at a discount. With the right guidance, you can find a UIT that will meet your needs for a dependable monthly income.

Understanding the Stock Market

A corporation is one of the most common business entities in America and around the world. They can range from a small enterprise that manufactures widgets to a large industry corporation like Coca Cola. Corporations issue stock to raise money. When you buy common shares in a company, you become a part owner of that company, along with other people and institutions, which all own shares of stock (equities) that have been issued. The shares you own can go up and down as investors buy and sell them depending upon the future outlook (forecast) of the corporation. As a shareholder, you receive quarterly updates on how your company is performing. In the stock market, unless you have large sums of money to buy huge amounts of shares, you are basically investing smaller shares for the long term ride, letting the professionals of the company hone their skills to maximize that corporations profits. Beware – the stock market can be a dangerous place to invest money unless you know what you are doing. Millions of dollars have been gained and lost in the stock market. Be prudent and careful as you invest your money in stocks, as there are many brokers and traders always looking to vanquish your hard earned money.

Not only can you earn profit from a rising share price, but you can also earn money from stocks by collecting dividends. If the corporation is profitable, you will receive a quarterly check for your shares of investment. Keep in mind that large corporations, that are well established like Wal-Mart and IBM, are more often profitable and pay a dividend. Smaller growing companies sometimes take awhile for you to reap a dividend down the road.

When a company offers shares to the public for the first time it is called an initial public offering (IPO). They then use the proceeds from the shares purchased to expand their business, do new research and development, or pay down on its debt. If the company needs more money to grow, later on they can issue additional shares in what is then termed a secondary offering. Shares of stock are usually purchased through a broker/brokerage firm that is a member of the exchange. Acting as agents, they charge a commission for their services. Commission rates are set by the investment firm, setting its rates according to the level of services it provides. A "discount" brokerage firm will usually offer lower rates and lower levels of service.

There are three main exchanges where buyers meet sellers. All exchanges must be registered with the Securities and Exchange Commission. They are:

1. **New York Stock Exchange (NYSE)** This exchange is the oldest, founded in 1792, and the most influential exchange. It is home to about 3000 of the largest and most well known companies in the United States.

2. **American Stock Exchange (AMEX)** This exchange is the second largest, and it resembles the NYSE except that it is smaller. AMEX is home to about 800 small and medium sized growth companies.

3. **Nasdaq National Market System (NASDAQ)** This exchange is known as National Association of Securities Dealers Automated Quotation System. It is a computerized stock quotation system providing subscribers instant information concerning thousands of stocks. Typically, NASDAQ features only the most actively traded over the counter (OTC) stocks.

Common Stock

Owners of common stock have voting rights in the corporation. As shareholders, they are entitled to declared dividends. They also have the right to buy and sell stock at will and are allowed to vote on matters affecting the corporation, they also receive annual reports. As an owner of common stock you benefit from dividends paid usually in cash or stock, and you have the potential for appreciation. The value of the stock in the corporation can increase if the company does well. It can also tank to the bottom if problems arise and bankruptcy occurs. (Which is happening to more and more companies these days). Be aware that picking the right company stock is not a perfect win every time.

Preferred Stock

Preferred stock is a mixed equity security, which has characteristics of both stocks and bonds. Dividends paid on preferred stock have a priority over payment of the common stock dividend. Dividends owned by preferred shareholders are fixed and do not fluctuate according to the corporation's profitability and earnings as does the common stock dividends. The dividends are paid at fixed rate and are stated as a percentage of par value. In the event of liquidation by the corporation, the preferred shareholders have a priority claim to the assets over the common stock shareholders, but are subordinate to the bondholders and creditors. Many investors are attracted to the preferred stocks, since they provide security and offer a stable income.

Different Categories of Stocks

Growth Stocks – These are stocks of relatively new and fast expanding companies.

Rapid Growth Stocks – These are stocks that are experiencing highly successful growth patterns, whose earnings per share have increased an average of 20 to 30 percent a year for the previous five years. (Ex.-Home Depot, Lowes)

Intermediate Growth Stocks – These stocks are well-established companies, they have a consistent growth of earnings and their earnings have increased an average of 10 to 20 percent a year for the previous 10 years. (Ex.-Walgreens, Pepsi Cola)

Slow Growth Stocks – These stocks, often called income, blue chip, low-growth stocks are some of the safest type of stocks you can purchase. They have earnings, which grow from 6 to 12 percent a year. (Ex.-General Electric, Colgate-Palmolive)

Income Stocks – These stocks are of established companies that have a history of paying good, solid dividends. (Ex.- Ameren UE, American Water Company)

Cyclical Stocks – These stocks rise and fall with the business cycle. Cyclical industries include steel, aluminum, automobiles, home building, machinery, travel and leisure.

Emerging Growth Stocks – These are companies whose earnings have increased an average of 30 to 60 percent a year for the past three years. They usually develop a unique or innovative product or service and they have had some gainful, initial beginning success. (Ex.-Google. com., Intel)

Foreign Stocks – These stocks are primarily in the Europe and Asian markets. They can be a very good place to invest. Most foreign stocks are sold in the form of an American depository receipts (ADRs). An ADR is a receipt for shares of the foreign-based corporation and is held in the vault at a U.S. Bank. As a service convenience, all dividends are converted from the home country currency into dollars before they are paid. Keep in mind, like any investments in foreign securities, your investments can alter by swings in the value of the U.S. dollar against foreign currencies. (Ex.-Nestle, Honda)

Dollar Cost Averaging

Dollar cost averaging (DCA) is a method of investing where you designate a specific dollar amount at a specific time, regardless of the stock or bond markets performance. It averages out the market fluctuations, encourages you to save on a consistent basis, reduces your average cost per share and you can authorize your bank to do an automatic draft payment to that invested account.

Investing in Mutual Funds for your Future

A mutual fund is a method of investing in the financial markets (stocks & bonds, etc.) with a pool of money contributed by a number of different investors. A professional fund manager buys and sells stocks according to the parameters set by the specific fund. Mutual funds provide diversification by investing in multiple companies within many different industries. As an investor, you own shares in the mutual fund in proportion to the money you invest, then you receive your proportionate share of any earnings on the investment of the funds involved.

I think mutual funds are one of the best ways to invest your money today. Why? Because they offer you the opportunity to invest in the stock market, without having to manage and select your portfolio, and they offer the potential for higher returns on your money versus most fixed rate investments. The potential returns can exceed taxes and the rate of inflation and while being convenient, mutual funds allow you to invest in the stock market with small amounts of money. Mutual funds offer the potential to make money in three ways:
1. **Dividends paid** on the earnings of the funds.
2. **Capital gains distribution** through any profits earned by the fund when they buy and sell stocks or bonds.

3. **Appreciation of shares** held over long-term period, through the increase in the value of the stocks and/or bonds owned by the fund. (Net Asset Value)

Stock Market Indexes

A stock market index is a list of stocks whose combined performance is tracked by investors as an indication of the health of a particular portion of the economy. The following are some of the best-known indexes:

Dow Jones Industrial Average – Tracks the stocks of 30 of America's most prestigious firms.

The Standard & Poors (S&P) 500 Index – Tracks the performance of some 500 large U.S. companies.

The Wilshire 5000 Index – Tracks the entire U.S. stock market.

The Russell 2000 Index – Tracks the smaller, faster growing companies.

The Morgan Stanley Select Emerging Markets Index – Tracks the companies in developing regions of the world, like Europe, Asia and South America.

There are two types of Mutual Funds and they are:

Closed-end funds – These funds sell a limited number of shares. They are traded on the stock exchange just like actual stocks.

Open-end funds – These funds sell as many shares as investors are willing to buy. They will buy shares back at any time. These shares are not traded on a stock exchange.

Different Categories of Mutual Funds

Money-market funds – They invest in short-term bonds issued by the U.S. government, large corporations, local government, states, and banking industries. They are considered a very safe investment with cash liquidity.

Corporate bond/Income funds – These funds invest in debt issued by companies that need to raise money. Primary objective of bond/fixed income funds is income generated from the interest paid on the loans. Usually a lower risk and less volatile investment, which helps guard against unexpected shifts in the stock market.

Small Cap funds – These stock mutual funds work with companies in small market capitalization, usually below $1 Billion. Some funds focus on start-up companies in emerging fields like technology or biotechnology.

Mid Cap funds – They fall between the large and small cap funds, generally having market capitalization between $1 Billion and $5 Billion. Mid cap stocks might be in utility, oil, gas and electric companies.

Large Cap funds – They specialize in stocks with a market value of more than $5 Billion. They focus on large well-established companies, like IBM, General Motors, Hewlitt Packard, which have lower risks than smaller cap companies.

Value funds – These funds have a strategy to purchase stocks in undervalued companies where prices are lower than they seem to be worth, which are currently out of favor, or have dropped in value.

U.S. Government funds – These funds purchase government securities such as U.S. Treasury bonds and guaranteed mortgage-backed securities (GNMAs), which are backed by the Federal government and other notes.

Index funds – These funds purchase shares in all of the stocks held by a particular stock market index, such as the S&P 500. They tend to outperform most mutual fund companies because of their lower management fees.

High Yield Bond funds – These funds, because they purchase lower rated corporate bonds (junk bonds), carry more risk than higher rate bond funds. But, they also generally offer a higher return on investment.

Growth funds – These are stock funds managed primarily in the pursuit of capital gains, so the fund manager takes the form of higher share prices versus the dividends paid by the company. The manager is looking for companies that are rapidly expanding due to economic, social or business trends. These funds are managed with such expertise they are growing quickly.

Aggressive Growth funds – The manager of such a fund buys stocks they think have the most exciting growth possibilities. They would include small cap stocks, companies developing new technologies, and stocks in companies where the business is likely to double or triple within a few years.

Specialized Sector funds – These funds specialize in stocks from a specific industry. Here, the fund manager is an expert on the companies in that industry; he understands the long-term growth prospects along with the social and business trends likely to affect it.

Balanced funds – These funds invest both stocks and bonds. It is a more conservative type of fund, which attempts to balance the safety of bonds along with the growth potential of stocks through a single investment. Typically they are 60% invested in stocks and 40% invested in bonds.

Tax-Free Mutual Bond funds – These bond funds are an IOU issued by a state, country, city, or local government, often driven to raise money for a specific purpose. They often pay slightly lower interest rates than government or corporate bonds. Of course the big draw is the interest from most municipal bonds is exempt from federal income taxes and even some bonds will offer tax-free bonds in the state where you live.

International funds – These funds are like any foreign investment in other regions of the world such as Japan, Korea, and Germany. They have the potential to grow rapidly and expand their markets as they try to keep up with the U.S. industry and our vortex for consumer spending. Again, you have currency risk, along with foreign economies, changing tax laws, political and business upheavals.

Advantages of Mutual Funds

Diversification – Investing all of your money in two to three stocks can be a risky planning program. If the stocks do poorly you can lose a lot of money. Mutual funds offer a wide variety of different securities representing mixed shares from different companies and even industries.

Low entry cost – You can get started investing in a mutual fund with relatively little money, either by a lump sum, voluntary, or systematic monthly contributions.

Professional Management – Most people don't have the time or want to take the time to learn and be disciplined in understanding the stock market. Let the full-time professional fund managers make the expert decisions about when to buy, sell or switch securities.

Tax Reporting – Your mutual fund sends you an annual statement indicating your income and any capital gains the fund may have accrued.

Shareholder Services – These services can offer check-writing privileges, ability to invest, withdraw, or move money via mail, telephone or Internet. Automatic payroll deductions, record keeping for filing your tax return, and access to reports about companies, funds and economic trends.

Liquidity – Ease to buy or sell an investment, as well as mutual funds can be cashed in quickly.

Convenience – Tracking your investments with companies in your portfolio is as easy as reading the daily newspaper. You will receive a fund statement each time you make a transaction and also the annual report on your fund's progress.

Growth Potential – Mutual funds have historically outperformed more conservative investments like money markets and bond programs. There is some risk but mutual funds offer a much better potential for growth than investments that are totally risk free.

Final Comments on Mutual Funds

- Mutual funds are a great tool to become "an owner, not a loaner." They give average American families the advantage of investing in the economy, via professional management, diversification and the opportunity to minimize risk.
- Invest for the long term. History shows that over time, stocks outperform other types of investments.
- Re-invest your dividends. Resist the temptation to withdraw money from dividends, and invest that added income back into the fund to build toward your financial security.
- Don't try to be an expert and anticipate "market ups" to only invest during that time period. Even the experts can't always pick the winners.
- Match your age and circumstances to the level of risk in your investments. When you're young you can afford to be more aggressive versus when you are older and approaching retirement your best option is a more conservative fund.
- Look carefully at the combination of investing in the long-term focus of an IRA by investing in mutual funds within your IRA.

Planning for Your Children's College Education

Planning ahead in the future for your children's education is many times scripted by hard decisions. How much do you need to invest? Where do you come up with the extra money from your tight budget to invest for college? How much will college education cost for my kids in 18-20 years? The most important decision you make will be a first step dedicated to putting "X" amount of money aside per month for your children's future college education. Keep in mind there are grants, funds and scholarships available, start looking at these opportunities when they are in their sophomore year. Attend High School Career nights, college fairs and even contact the schools you are considering to see what financial aid programs are available. The other key decision to consider is what kind of institution will they be selecting:

- **Top Ranked College/Ivy League School** – Think higher costs, tuition, fees, more money required for monthly investments.
- **Public University within your state** – This can be affordable and sometimes one of the best solutions to attending a four year institution.
- **Public University outside your state** – You have to pay out-of-state tuition fees, which can add up quickly along with all the other fees. Plan for more dollars invested per month for this education, but still affordable with use of grants or scholarships.
- **Junior or Community College** – Depending upon how your child's grades, study habits, self-esteem, and attitude for college permeates, this can sometimes be a great starting plan. The student lives at home, probably works a part-time job and with discipline and hard work they know they can make it in college.
- **Technical or Vocational Schools** – Don't count these trade schools out, many offer diverse programs and skill sets to choose a variety of careers that create comfortable and excellent paying incomes.

College Savings Programs

Education IRAs were created as part of the Taxpayer Relief Act of 1997. It allows you to save up to $500 per year per child under the age of 18 to help pay for college expenses. The money invested into the Education IRA does not generate a deduction, but the principal and all income, along with capital gains, can be used tax-free to pay for college education areas such as tuition, books, room and board, and other related fees.

Section 529 College Savings Plans. These are state sponsored educational savings programs that allow parents, relatives, and friends to invest in a fund for your children's college education. The parent must set up the account for the child with a mutual fund or brokerage firm. The state usually designates a specific investment company to offer the plan to that state's residents. Under this plan you can contribute a lot more money into the 529, unlike other college savings programs. For more information you can find details at this web site: (smartmoney. com/college/) **Note**: Make sure you have fully funded your retirement plan as best you can before opening a 529. Ask grandparents to open the 529 instead of you. (You can still contribute up to $11,000 a year or $22,000 for married couples without gift-tax consequences). A 529 plan owned by grandparents doesn't affect your child's financial eligibility. If a parent owns it, up to 5.6% of assets in the 529 plan will be assessed for financial need.

There are other means of investing for your children's education. I recommend you consult a financial advisor in this area once you have decided the amount of money you can divert toward college investments. I believe the key is starting early, like upon the birth of your child, and contributing at least $500 a year in an investment vehicle.

Investment and Financial Web Sites:

(moneycentral.com)	(quicken.com)
(multex.com)	(money.com)
(morningstar.com)	(cbsmarketwatch.com)
(bondsonline.com)	(investingbonds.com)

Software Programs to help in the Personal Finance area include:

Quicken	Kiplinger's Simple Money
Managing Your Money	Microsoft Money

Money Magazine – (800-633-9970) web site @ (money.com) To subscribe: (subsvcs@money.customersvc.com)

Recommended financial books include:

Get a Financial Life: Personal Finance in Your Twenties & Thirties, by Beth Kobliner. Publisher is Fireside
Personal Finance for Dummies, by Eric Tyson. IDG Books

Making the Most of Your Money, by Jane Bryant Quinn. Simon & Schuster

The Road to Wealth, by Suze Orman. Riverhead Books

Investing for Dummies, by Eric Tyson, Wiley Publishing Inc.

The Complete Idiot's Guide to Managing Your Money, by Robert K. Heady & Christy Heady with Hugo Ottolenghi, Alpha Publishing.

Rich Dad's Guide to Investing, by Robert T. Kiyosaki, Warner Business Books.

References:

(Prudential.com)   (Fool.com)
(Money.com)   (MSN.com)
(PrestigeAdvisors.com)   (Fidelity.com)
(Primerica.com)   (CashCowMag.com)
(Hoovers.com)   (Investopodia.com)
(Bloomberg.com)   (VanGuard.com)

NOTES:

NOTES:

7

INSURANCE –
PROTECT WHAT YOU OWN

An important part of life for the next 50 years will be protecting what you own by means of insurance. Your goal with insurance is to establish the coverage you'll need to protect yourself, your family and the "gold mine" you are building against financial disaster, yet to spend as little as possible

doing so. Take any savings you earn and apply that toward your retirement planning as we discussed in Chapter Six.

The need for insurance is to protect you from financial loss due to illness, accident, or natural disaster. You may have experienced a major loss already. A burglary in your apartment, a fire in your home, a car accident, some personal property that was stolen. In just seconds or minutes an unforeseen incident can happen, leaving much of what you have worked very hard to acquire totally wiped out. The potential for loss makes life, disability and health insurance along with homeowner's and auto insurance a necessity. In this chapter I hope to educate you in the importance of protecting what you own.

Auto Insurance

Car insurance is critical for anyone who drives a car, regardless of your driving ability and experience. In case you injure someone in an accident you need some form of coverage. In the state of Missouri you are required to have car insurance. Premiums (the charge you pay for all types of insurance) can vary tremendously from one insurance company to another. Let's take a look at the different types of coverage an auto policy might cover:

Bodily Injury Liability – This covers injuries that happen to passengers in your car or other cars, or to pedestrians when you are responsible for causing the accident. It may also cover you when driving someone else's car with their permission.

Property Damage Liability – This covers you for damages to another person's property, such as another person's car or possessions that was harmed by your car.

Uninsured Motorists (UM) – This covers you and your family if you are injured in an accident that was caused by someone else not covered by auto insurance, including a hit-an-run driver.

Underinsured Motorist (UIM) – This covers you if the other party does not have enough BI/Liability to cover your injuries if they are at fault in the accident. Only a few companies in Missouri are offering this coverage right now, UIM is not listed in MO laws.

Medical Payments, or Personal Injury Protection (PIP) – These payments cover you and your passengers for injuries sustained in an auto accident, regardless of who is at fault. It's often optional, but worth considering.

Collision – This covers the cost of repair or replacing your car after an accident, regardless of who is at fault.

Comprehensive – This protects your car, not you or your family. It covers damages for most circumstances other than collision, including theft, vandalism, fire, hail and animal contact.

Towing – This covers the cost of having your car hauled to a service station. Some plans might provide an emergency road service program, check with your agent on what they offer.

Rental Reimbursement – This provides coverage for your rental car for a specified length of time while your car is being repaired.

Remember that your driving record can affect your premiums. Insurance companies will look at your driving past to check on any tickets for speeding, DUIs, reckless driving, and road rage. On a single car policy with just one ticket it can raise rates 40% or more, if you have one DUI or three speeding tickets you might be looking at a 150% rate increase. Drive carefully, don't speed and don't drink and drive... it's not worth it.

Auto insurance is important but also be aware of ways to save money:

- **Shop a couple insurance agents.** Don't be shy about "shopping around" for the best deal. Be aware that property/casualty insurance agents (which sell homeowner's, rental, and automobile insurance) make their living by commissions. Ask your family and friends for referrals, it does make a difference finding the right person you feel comfortable with.
- **Use one company/agent to buy your insurance.** Sometimes packaged (bundled) home and auto insurance can provide the best economical costs. By having your home and car insured by the same company you can save money.
- **Get the highest deductible you can afford.** With certain types of insurance coverage, you have to pay a fixed dollar amount of the costs before your insurance kicks in. This fixed amount is known as a deductible. See what you can afford and weigh the options to see where you can lower your costs.
- **Be a good driver.** The difference in costs between a single person/family with no moving violations versus a single person/family with one or more violations, considering all factors equal, can be alarming. Make sure to drive defensively, drive the speed limit, don't drink and drive, and don't take needless traffic risks.
- **Contact companies that sell directly to the consumers.** Some auto insurance companies don't sell through agents but sell directly to consumers. These firms charge less because they have no sales force, have no commissions to pay, thus they can charge less. Example: GEICO (800-841-3000) or AMICA (800-992-6422)
- **Try the Consumer Reports Buying Guide.** This guide offers ratings of companies that sell auto insurance as well as health, homeowner's and life insurance.
- **Check complaint reports from Missouri Department of Insurance.** This is another guide to check on ratings of companies that sell auto insurance. (insurance.mo.gov)
- **Be aware that sports/specialty cars costs more.** These types of cars, especially with bigger engines cost more to insure and repair.

- **Safety features in cars can save money**. Safety features such as air bags, anti-theft devices, car alarms, OnStar Service program, stability control, and anti-lock brakes can qualify for additional discounts. Always ask about any extra discounts with your agent.

Homeowners Insurance

When you own a home, you will be required to get coverage on the building by the lender. Homeowner's insurance covers the cost of rebuilding or repairing your home if it's destroyed or damaged by disasters such as theft, fire, snow or wind storm damage. Most homeowners insurance protects three major areas: the dwelling (home's structure), the contents of the home and liability to other people and other people's property. Let's take a look at all three:

The Dwelling or home structure. You need to buy enough insurance to cover the full cost of rebuilding your home. To determine this seek the help of your insurance agent, they have formulas to help determine the cost per square feet in your home area. The costs to rebuild your home is known as your home's replacement cost.

The Contents of the home. This covers your "personal property" inside the home. Make sure your personal property insurance covers you for the replacement costs, not actual cash value of your home's contents. You may have a 7 year old TV set that is destroyed, you will want to buy a new one in its place (not the 7 year old set) and that will cost considerably more than the insurance company would give you for the old one. I suggest writing down a list of all your belongings, the purchase date and price of stereos, televisions, furniture, computers, artwork, DVD players, musical instruments, and major appliances. Keep a copy at your work office and one at home in a file cabinet or fireproof safe. This inventory list can come in handy if you ever need to file a claim. Start the list young, as you grow older keep it updated and store it in the same place all the time. Update as needed with each new major purchase.

Damage you do to other people and other people's property. This liability insurance will cover your for damage you cause outside or inside your home. If the neighbor comes over for BBQ and falls through a rotted lumber piece on your deck, breaks his leg, your liability insurance will cover his medical bills and other costs if you're responsible for his injury. If you have a pet, your policy will cover the damage the pet does to people or property. Be careful to get plenty of coverage in this area because people everywhere are "sue happy" and $500,000 may not be enough. To get an idea, add up all your major assets including your cars, your possessions and your financial investments. The amount of liability insurance should exceed these amounts.

Homeowner's Policies

There are seven standard types of homeowner policies. For most people insuring a home you will choose from one of the policies below:

HO-1 (The Basic Form) This covers the dwelling, other structures on the premise, and personal property against losses from the following eleven types of peril:

- Lightning or fire
- Explosion
- Windstorm or hail damage
- Aircraft
- Vehicles
- Smoke
- Theft
- Vandalism or malicious mischief
- Riot or civil commotion
- Damage by glass or glazing material that is part of a building
- Volcanic eruptions

HO 2 (The Broad Form) This is the basic homeowner form with extras, along with dwelling and personal property it includes the eleven above perils plus six more:

- Weight of snow, ice or sleet
- Falling objects, including trees
- Electrical surge damage
- Freezing of plumbing, heating or air conditioning system or automatic fire protection system, or of a household appliance
- Sonic Boom
- Three categories of water-related damage from home utilities and/or appliances

HO 3 (The Special Form) This insures your personal property against loss by the same perils included in HO 2, but adds more coverage. HO 3 provides the most complete coverage for dwelling and other structures. It insures the home and other structures against risk of direct physical loss. Such as if a vehicle does damage to your fence, walkway, or driveway. It does not cover the following:

- Gradual, expected or preventable losses, such as wear and tear, rust, mold, wet or dry rot, contamination
- Insects, vermin, rodents, or domestic animals
- Vandalism if the dwelling has been vacant for more than 30 consecutive days
- Any loss from collapse, other than provided under the additional coverage section
- Flood, earthquake, and nuclear accidents
- Contamination including but not limited to toxic chemicals and gases
- Losses by faulty or defective planning, zoning, surveying, design, construction, renovation, remodeling, grading or construction materials used, or maintenance

HO 4 (The Renter Form) This is renter's coverage insurance and usually covers your possessions under the 17 listed perils.

HO 5 (The Mega-coverage Plan) This covers it all but is way too expensive, instead add supplementary coverage to HO 3.

HO 6 (The Condo Unit Owner Form) This insures personal property against all of the 17 perils found on the Broad Form. Condo Insurance is usually very affordable.

HO 8 (The Modified Basic Form) This is for older homes, which may have some historic or architectural aspects. It covers the dwelling and personal property from the 11 perils. It differs from the HO 1 because it covers repairs or actual cash values (ACV), not rebuilding costs. Partial losses are paid on an ACV basis. Talk to your agent to find out more on this form if you are buying an older home.

Replacement Value and Replacement Cost

Make sure you have enough insurance to cover the cost of rebuilding your home, not the current market value of the home. If the limit of your homeowner's coverage is based on your mortgage, make sure it is enough to cover the current cost of rebuilding. In most cases you buy insurance for at least 80% of your home's replacement value. If you buy less, you lose the right to collect full replacement value of the insured property, even for a partial loss. Ask your agent to help you with this formula. The best method is to buy a guaranteed replacement cost policy, which will pay up to 50% more than the face value of the policy to rebuild your home.

Liability Coverage

This is a very important area to look at. Liability coverage on a homeowner policy will protect you against liabilities up to the value of the house itself. Many people tend to use their homeowner policy as their main protection from civil lawsuits. Most homeowner policies pay up to $100,000 (some are $500,000) each time someone makes a legitimate liability claim against you. If the liability claim against you is more than $100,000, you would have to pay the difference. With the American way of being "sue happy" these days, you need to have proper coverage. I recommend adding a rider to the policy to compensate where you feel most comfortable. Talk to your agent about having enough liability protection. Because the cost of hiring an attorney to defend yourself in a civil lawsuit can easily reach $10,000 to $25,000 fast. Another reason liability insurance is valuable, it covers the cost of mounting your legal defense. Compare and critique policies that individually fit your program to obtain the coverage at premiums you can afford.

Renter's Insurance

If you are renting, get basic renter's insurance. It is very affordable, it can average about $200 a year for a policy that gives you up to $40,000 worth of coverage on your belongings, and another $300,000 of liability insurance, with a $250 deductible. Don't be stupid or frugal, if you're renting then get some insurance.

Homeowners Insurance Advice

- If you have a standard homeowners policy, you probably don't need to purchase any separate policy to cover credit card charges if someone steals your credit card and makes purchases. Most HO policies will pay up to $500 in charges.
- A personal articles rider or floater can be expensive. Add this coverage only if the loss would be a large financial one, versus just a sentimental one.

- Home improvements such as replacing old electrical wiring in the home or upgrading the plumbing system might entitle you to a discount because your house has become more fireproof.
- Installing a "home security" system can usually bring discounts. Some insurance firms offer up to a 10 to 20 percent discount for sophisticated sprinkler and burglar alarm systems connected to a local fire, police or security station.
- Multiple policies are important to keep in mind if you purchase an umbrella policy with the homeowners and auto insurance together, you may be eligible for a 5 to 15 percent discount on your premiums. Ask your agent about this program.
- Shoot a video or take digital pictures of your belongings (including furniture, jewelry, cars and special items) as a visual record and store in a safe deposit box or another secure location outside your home.
- Stop smoking! Some companies offer a small discount if everyone in the home is a non-smoker.
- Shop around for insurance rates, and the right company (should be of A, AA AAA rating). Here is a good web site to look at on the Internet from the Insurance Information Institute. (iii.org)

Life Insurance

Life insurance is a key important structural foundation in your financial planning area, for you and your family. Life insurance basically protects against the risk of you dying too soon. It pays a death benefit to someone (named beneficiary) when you die. The purpose of life insurance is like a substitute for income. In the event of your premature death, you leave your family or business unprotected (exposed) to certain financial risks. Your earning potential in a lifetime is what you are paying to protect. Financial risks upon your death might include burial expenses, loss of family income, paying off debts, loss of business profits, paying estate taxes and limited college fund potential for your children.

The loss of that earning power through early death is what you are paying to protect. In most cases where today women are in the work force, if your wife is earning money she should have life insurance to protect you also. Burial expenses and child care if a spouse passes is still a factor to deal with.

Note: In talking to a number of life insurance agents I discovered it is vitally important to get a life insurance policy once you are working and established. As they mentioned *"get it while you can"* because you never know when an illness or disease (like MS or diabetes) might strike. Don't wait until you are in your forties. Many people don't think they need life insurance, but you might not be insurable later in life. Your goal might be a $250,000 to $500,000 term insurance policy at a young age. *Don't wait 'till it's too late.*

Types of Insurance

Insurance companies that offer life insurance all basically see the same principle of insurance to issue a policy in the event of a death. But be aware they can all have their own set of incentives, which reflects upon the quality of the policies they offer. Let's look at few options:

Government Programs – These Federal and State government programs provide insurance for millions of people. In some cases, they provide insurance where some private companies cannot or will not offer insurance. Examples would include Medicare, Social Security, Department of Veterans Affairs (VA), State offered disability, workers compensation and unemployment insurance.

Stock Companies – These are companies owned by shareholders who are in business to earn a profit. They are usually larger, strong financial companies that can offer extremely competitive policies. Examples include Equitable, Allstate, Travelers, Chubb, and International Group.

Cooperatives – These companies are groups that write together (coop) to provide insurance for themselves. They hire professional managers to run the administrative tasks of collecting premiums and paying claims. The best example of a cooperative is Blue Cross/Blue Shield.

Mutual Companies – These companies are insurers organized in a mutual alliance and are owned by their policyholders. They work on the premise that if the mutual company does well you benefit, if they do poorly you can see higher premiums. They work to keep expenses low, hopefully pay few death claims and thus create superior investment performance. They build up surpluses over the years and can be very strong financially. Examples here are State Farm, John Hanock, Prudential, and Northwestern Mutual.

Different Way Life Insurance can be Offered

When looking at the kind of policy you'll need from a company, there are a number of ways to obtain insurance and they are:

1. **Through your employer.** When you become a member of a labor union or employee of a company, many times you qualify automatically for whatever insurance that organization offers to its employees/members. You'll need to check with the Human Resources department to see what coverage for life insurance is offered to you. In many cases it is a small amount, $10,000 to $25,000 upon your death.

2. **Insurance agents.** These sellers of insurance are state licensed. They work to determine your needs and then find the policy that best provides the coverage you need for the lowest premium. In return they receive a commission for the sale of the policy, and often also get a renewal commission for every year that you keep the policy in force.

3. **Insurance brokers.** Brokers are employed by the insurance company to find the best policy for the most competitive price. They may purchase a policy from an agent or directly from the insurance company. They earn a commission based upon the premium you pay. They also receive yearly renewals as long as the policy is in force.

4. **Independent "Quote Services."** This is a new kind of insurance broker, you call in to a toll-free number, and a service representative takes your age, your health condition and the coverage you want. Then they resource a database of term insurance companies and mail you out 4 to 5 quotes, with the lowest premiums. If you like one of the quotes, you buy the policy through the quote service. Examples here are Selectquote, Termquote, and Insurance Quote.

5. **Insurance Advisors.** Unlike agents or brokers, who earn a commission, advisors charge a flat fee for services. They work with insurance companies that pay no or very low commissions to salespeople and thus offer higher returns on programs.

6. **Direct Marketing companies.** I discussed these companies earlier. They have no expensive sales force; they offer you coverage through the mail or by phone. These policies can be less expensive but you have no direct contact with a company representative.

Read the final contract carefully and then make the decision your-self.

Different Types of Life Insurance

Lets look next at a number of different types of life insurance. When you get down to it there are basically two categories, term insurance and whole life (cash value) insurance.

Term Insurance policies insure you for a stated time period or term, for a specific amount of money (death benefit). An example would be if you purchase a 20-year term policy for $250,000, and you die within the 20-year period, your beneficiaries would receive $250,000. Once you live past the 20 years, the policy is over, becomes null and void.

Whole Life Insurance (also known as Cash Value) provides a death benefit along with a savings/investment plan. Whole life and universal life fall in this category.

Term Insurance

Term insurance in my opinion is the best type of life insurance. It's the least expensive and purest insurance to get if all you're interested in is providing your family (wife and kids) an income upon your unforeseen death. Term insurance policies are a great fit for the typical families financial life cycle. Years ago I had an insurance agent explain to me this very important principle:

"The Principle of Decreasing Responsibility"

Basically, it is a method of looking at an average American family including mom, dad and two to four children. The principle works like this:

When you're young – You have young children to support, you are paying on a home mortgage, you have maybe accumulated some debt, yet you haven't had the time to accumulate much cash. This is the time when the death of a spouse (breadwinner-either mom or dad), would be devastating. Now is when you need an insurance policy and it is of the utmost importance. Term insurance lets you buy low cost protection for high dollar coverage upon your death. Take the extra money you save and apply that to your current investment program.

When you're older – You most probably have fewer dependents, and less financial responsibilities. The kids have grown up, the mortgage is paid off or significantly reduced, and much of your routine payments have gone away. You have followed a disciplined financial savings plan and now you have significant accumulated cash. So once you have the cash, your need for "death protection" is reduced dramatically.

Source: Internet web site of Primerica at (primerica.com)

Keep in mind that if you're like most people, your major goal is to accumulate money for a secure and happy retirement. Life insurance is simply the vehicle/tool to protect your family until you build up the nest egg (cash). Everyone's needs and circumstances are different and we all travel our own life course, but in theory this is a great plan!

A term life policy lasts for a set period (term) of years. When you buy a 20-year term policy you pay premiums for 20 years unless during that 20-year term you die, then the policy pays the face amount to your beneficiary.

Let's look at four types of Term Insurance:

1. **Annual Renewable Term** – When you start, you essentially buy one year's insurance at a specified price. The next year, because you are one year older, the cost of the insurance increases. This type of insurance is very affordable in the early years but becomes more expensive as you get older.

2. **Level Term** – This is probably the most popular and provides a consistent amount of insurance through the policy period. You buy for a specific number of years (10-30) and your premium remains the same level for the period. It averages the cost of insurance over the period of the policy.

3. **Modified Level Term** – This is a variation on level term insurance. It usually has a modified level term, so that your first year premium is higher to include policy expenses, thereafter it has a reduced level premium for the remainder of the policy.

4. **Decreasing Term** – This allows you to start with a specific face amount, paying a level premium throughout the term of the policy, but the face amount decreases as you get older. Some policies might offer level term for 10-20 years, and then convert to decreasing term the last 5 years of the policy. Ask your agent for more details.

Keep in mind some term policies are also convertible, meaning they may be replaced for another type of insurance (such as Whole Life). Choosing convertible term insurance is one way to make sure you will be able to get permanent coverage at a later time, without proving that you are still insurable.

How Much Insurance do you Need?

The amount of insurance you need will vary depending upon your individual needs. One thing I came across in my research studies was that most people don't have enough life insurance coverage. Consult your insurance agent to help evaluate your needs. Here are some guidelines I came across that you might consider. You will need five to ten times your annual salary, depending upon your cash assets, number of dependents in the family and your designated lifestyle. One insurance agent suggested at least $500,000 on the main breadwinner (assuming you're married with children), plus $50,000 added to the face amount for each child. Make sure when you buy coverage, you buy only one policy. Separate policies with extra coverage amounts mean costly additional expense fees.

Whole Life Insurance

Whole Life insurance or cash value policies do double duty as investment vehicles. They bundle a life insurance policy along with a form of savings or investment feature. You are required to buy both benefits and although it is more expensive, it offers more value. Each year some of the premium goes into an investment type account, if you cancel the policy before you die you will collect that portion of the money. Whole life policy is sometimes called straight life or permanent life, a protection you can keep as long as you live. The following are some characteristics of Whole Life insurance:

- Enables you to pay the same premium over the years, averaging the cost of the policy over your lifetime.
- It builds a **cash value,** which is a sum of money that grows over the years and is tax-deferred.
- If you have a temporary crisis and are unable to pay the premiums, you can use the cash value in the policy to pay your premiums for a period of time.

- If you cancel the policy, you receive a **lump sum** equal to this amount and you pay taxes on it if the cash value plus any dividends exceeds the sum of the premiums you paid.
- The **face amount** in a whole life policy is constant, and this amount is paid to your beneficiary if you die at any time while the policy is in effect.
- The policy matures when you reach age 100. If you live to be 100, premium payments cease, and the policy's cash value will be equal to the face amount.
- Whole life policies offer a **guaranteed interest** rate on any loan you take out against the cash value of the policy. So if you need to borrow money against the policy for an emergency you may do so. Somewhere down the road the money will be made up or the value of the face amount will be decreased accordingly.
- A **participating (par) policy** is issued by a mutual life insurance company, and the policyholders receive dividends.
- A **nonparticipating (non-par)** policy is issued by a stock life insurance company, and does not pay dividends.

Universal Life Insurance

This type of whole life policy is a combination program, having features of term insurance and cash value insurance. In the universal life policy, the owner has the added benefit of flexible premium payments, meaning you can pay any time, any amount, subject to minimums set by the insurance company. The cash value the policy generates is based upon the premiums paid and on the interest earned. So the extra money you pay is put into an investment account that earns you a variable rate (but a guaranteed minimum) depending upon the performance of the insurance company's investments. The insurance company deducts money from the fund each month to cover the cost of the insurance and expenses. Other benefits include the ability to change the death benefit and premiums or borrow money from the account.

Variable Universal Life Insurance

This insurance program combines the features of a variable policy with a universal policy by giving the policy owner a minimum face value guarantee, the use of separate account for the cash value, and the benefit of flexible premium payments. Rather than earning a fixed interest rate of the cash value, the value of the investment is variable, depending upon the investment returns of stocks and bond funds managed by the life insurance company. Variable universal life is as much an investment tool as a true protection vehicle. The cost of variable universal life is too uncertain for many people because of the open-ended method of premium payments.

Other life insurance policies to consider include:

Modified Life – This policy is a whole life product purchased at a very low premium for a short time frame (usually 3 to 10 years), followed by a higher premium for the life of the policy. Cash value builds a lot slower in this type of program.

Limited-Payment Life – This allows you to pay premiums for a specific number of years (usually 7 to 20 years), and then they stop. Premiums are higher in this program, but cash values build faster as a result.

Single-Payment Life – This policy is paid in one lump sum premium payment. It can be thousands of dollars, but you never make any more payments the rest of your life. Be aware of the tax assessments if you want to draw money from the cash value that builds up.

Joint Life – This policy is a contract written with two or more persons named as the insureds. Some programs pay on the death of the first insured only, others pay on both deaths. A variation on this program is last survivor policy, which pays the insured amount not to the beneficiaries of the first insured to die, but to the beneficiaries of the last one to die.

Adjustable Life – This policy allows you to make changes to the policy's face amount, length of protection and premium, without having to fill out a new application or have another policy issued. The theory here is flexibility to convert from term insurance to a whole life without adding, dropping or exchanging policies. Ask your agent for more details and options with adjustable life insurance.

Credit Life – This policy can be written as an individual credit life policy so that in the event of your death, outstanding balances on your credit card debt will be paid in full. It is usually written in "decreasing term" insurance, which grows smaller as the amount of debt shrinks. Theses contracts are usually added to the payment of major purchases, such as a car or appliance. The insurance premium is financed along with the item being purchased. I share this type of insurance for your knowledge, but I don't recommend it.

Accelerated Death Benefit Life – This new form of life insurance is made to access your death benefit while you are still living. It's designed for people with terminal diseases such as AIDS or cancer that requires costly treatments. These programs, also known as Living Benefit policies, will make payments while you are alive under these circumstances:

- You are diagnosed as terminally ill, and you have a doctor's confirmation in writing that you have only weeks or months to live.
- If you need long-term care in a nursing home or at your personal residence.
- If you are diagnosed with a catastrophic disease or illness that is accumulating large medical bills. The policy will list specific diseases and surgeries covered.

Annuities

Annuities are a little different than whole life or term insurance policies. Although they are underwritten by life insurance companies, they pay a regular stream of income while you live, usually after you retire, instead of paying you a lump sum when you die. They are very popular among people fifty years and older. Annuities provide an advantage of tax-deferred compounding on the investment portion of the account. Annuities have a life insurance component, they will pay your beneficiary (if you die before receiving payments) on the money you paid into the program plus any interest earned. There are two basic types of annuities and they are:

Deferred Annuity – These are purchased by younger people who want to save tax deferred money for many years, then transition to a "paid income" once they retire. They can be purchased with regular monthly premiums or with one lump sum, called a single-premium deferred annuity (SPDA). Most companies will ask for at least $2,500, but prefer to start with $10,000 or more on the lump sum payment.

Immediate Annuity – These are purchased with lump sum of money and work to generate a monthly income payout immediately. Generally theses are purchased by people in retirement, who use money from their pension plan, IRA, Keogh plan, or other investments they have accumulated over the years. You work with the insurance company to determine the level of monthly income depending upon how long you want to receive payments in relation to the total lump sum of money you put forth.

You have two annuity options to work with:

1. **Fixed Dollar Annuity** – Basically you give the insurance company your money and they guarantee to pay you a fixed amount of interest on the money you give them. The insurance company is investing in bonds or mortgages and following a conservative approach. But is doesn't matter to you how good or bad the investment does, you receive the same payment no matter what happens.

2. **Variable Annuity** – This offers a potential for higher returns, yet greater risk. This annuity gives you a choice among different bonds, stocks and other money-market portfolios. Your return is not guaranteed, but rather rides on the rewards of the investments you have chosen. If you tend to select companies with proven performance, in the long term you would be better investing in a variable annuity versus a fixed dollar annuity.

Disability Income Insurance

One final area to review is disability insurance. You probably think it will never happen to you, but...what if... you have an accident at work, you suffer a premature heart attack or stroke, or you are diagnosed with a debilitating illness? The odds are higher for you to achieve one of the above then for you to die. Life insurance protects you in case you die, disability insurance protects you in case you live, but become disabled. If you can't work or no longer earn a living, who will pay the bills? Will your family survive this type of crisis? I want you to be knowledgeable so **YOU** can make a qualified decision when it comes around (especially once you're married with children).

Disability insurance is a type of health insurance, which provides weekly or monthly pay benefits to replace a portion of the earnings you lose when you're unable to work because of an injury or illness. If you decide not to have disability insurance, you will need to rely on other resources to counter the effects of a disability. They could come from:

- Your cash savings or emergency fund.
- Your equity in your home, also be aware that long-term disability could force you to sell your house.
- Planned investments, and by starting to invest young (early in life), you could have sufficient money to draw from.
- Government programs, we will take a look at social security disability payments.
- Having to borrow money from family, friends or other sources.

Disability Programs at Work

If you're employed, ask the Human Resources department about work-related benefits in a group disability plan. These group benefit plans are usually short-term, up to a year or less, and only cover a percentage of lost income. Ask at work if they offer:

Short-term disability (STD). These group policies provide for short elimination periods (usually 30 days or less) along with short benefit periods (usually 6 months to one year).

Long-term disability (LTD). These policies provide for longer elimination periods (usually 90 days or 6 months) and typically longer benefits than short-term. Each policy can be different depending upon the insurance carrier.

Accidental Death & Dismemberment (AD&D). This coverage is provided as part of a group insurance contract. If you have an accident resulting in death or loose part of a limb that is work related certain lump sum payments are paid out under these group policies.

Workers Compensation Programs

Workers compensation provides a source of disability income benefits, but only if your sickness or accident is job-related. These benefits are paid when you are unable to perform all or part of your regular job duties. Compensation is paid in four designated classes of disability which are: permanent total, temporary total, permanent partial, and temporary partial. Your human resources administrator should supply you with all the guidelines once an accident or sickness occurs.

Association Disability Insurance

If you are a member of an association like the American Bar Association, they offer group association disability income to their members.

Because it serves a large group of people in the association, costs can be lower. Programs work on particular age brackets such as member between the ages of 25 to 35, 35 to 45, and 45 to 60. Premiums are not guaranteed, and as with all insurance these days, expect rate increases yearly.

Disability Insurance from an Insurance Company

Typically, individual disability insurance plans can be very complicated. Seek an insurance agent expert as you look to purchase your own disability insurance. Here are a couple types of disability insurance:

Occupational coverage. This provides payment for disability coming from accidents occurring on or off the job.

Non-occupational coverage. This provides payment only for disability that is not work related.

Residual disability coverage. This provides income benefits that are triggered by a loss of pre-disability income. They offer an incentive for the insured person to return to work, because benefits will continue in proportion to his/her loss of income.

Remember the younger you get insurance the better off you will be, simply because the older you are the more insurance guidelines you have to follow.

Social Security Coverage

You may or may not be able to count on social security disability income benefits. It can be very difficult to qualify for benefits and when they do finally come, they're not that great. The disability benefit social security pays out to you is equal to your primary insurance amount (PIA), which is based on your earnings history (years of employment) and the taxes you have paid. This benefit can be reduced by moneys paid out to you under state unemployment plans or worker's compensation. The program pays four types of benefits:

1. Disability benefits to workers
2. Medicare benefits
3. Retirement benefits to workers and their dependents
4. Survivors benefits to a worker's family

Qualification for disability income benefits from social security requires the following:

- You have fully insured and disability insured status,
- You are under the age of 65, and
- You have satisfied a five-month elimination period followed by submission of an application for benefits.

Note: After age 65 disability benefits cease and retirement benefits begin.

Along with the above requirements, a worker must meet the social security definition of *total disability,* defined as: "The inability to engage in any substantial gainful activity by reason of any medically determined physician or mental impairment which can be expected to result in death or last for at least 12 months."

The entire process is very strenuous, and in the final analysis the average out-pay for a social security benefit in 2004 would be maybe $500 to $800 per month. Not quite enough to live on, heh?

In summary, my main point is if you have a disability, it can be catastrophic financially. Look seriously at having a couple solutions available for disability income such as: through your work or member association, individual policy and/or social security disability benefits.

Wills

What is a will and what is it good for? A will is basically a set of written instructions as to what should be done with your property after you die. If you don't have a will in place you don't suffer, your heirs do! A will specifies those people (your family members) who will receive your property in the amounts you decide to disperse. It also designates shares (amounts) of your property to each one and describes what guidelines under which they should occur. Preparing a will is a structurally important part of meeting your financial responsibilities. If you have a will you can:

- Avoid family and friends needlessly worrying, bickering and fighting.
- Avoid intestacy (meaning you have died without a will and now the state you live in has their own set of rules on how your property is divided).
- Appoint guardians (keepers) for your minor children.
- Create trusts for tax savings and asset management.

- Name the executor of your estate.
- Make specific bequests to loved ones.
- Reduce estate litigation and other attorney fees.
- Provide for sale of assets, during estate administration.
- Provide for children by a previous marriage.

In all the literature I read 7 out of 10 Americans die without a will. Don't be foolish and be one of those 7 unfortunate people. I recommend you spend a couple hundred dollars, hire an attorney to draw up your will. The fees to hire an attorney should range between $100 and $500 to draw up a basic will that will function as a starting point.

For those wanting to do their own written wills there are many books on how to write a will. Software packages are also available for around $50. If it is just you and the wife working on your first wills, after you print all the documents, check on the guidelines for witnesses you'll need, and then have a lawyer or estate planner review the paperwork.

There are two types of wills:

1. **Holographic handwritten wills** – Only a small portion of states recognize handwritten wills these days. Check carefully if you are working with anyone with a handwritten will. Most states that do identify these wills do so only under limited circumstances and only for smaller estates.
2. **Witnessed wills** – All states recognize the validity of a written will that is witnessed and signed in accordance with their state guidelines.

Note: Remember wills have to be in writing and should be properly witnessed by two to three people who will not benefit from the will. Spoken words on a deathbed have no legal standing in court.

Appointing an Executor

The executor of your estate is a key person. Choose wisely when naming an executor. It is a task driven job, which I will point out shortly. I recommend you choose a spouse, an adult child, a close friend or relative over a lawyer, simply because they will work more diligently in a loving manner than a lawyer, and usually not charge for their services. These are the duties of an executor:

- Must obtain the original copy of the will and submit it to probate court for approval and validity.
- Required to publish death notice for a specified length of time.
- Open a checking account on behalf of the estate and maintain records of all transactions.
- Must inventory, appraise and safeguard all assets of the estate.
- Must apply for all appropriate death benefits, such as social security, Veterans Administration, pension plans, labor unions and any other organizations.
- Must pay all outstanding debts of the deceased.
- Must file and pay local, state, federal income and estate taxes.
- May be required to submit a final accounting of records to the court.
- Must distribute all remaining assets according to the terms of the will.

Terms to be familiar with include:

Testator – the person whose will it is.

Executor – Person or persons who will administer your estate.

Specific bequests – These are gifts of personal property to a friend, a gift of cash to a charity or alma mater. They are listed to specific people for designated (cherished) items.

General bequests – This is a gift that doesn't specify the source of funds it comes from.

Residual estate – What remains of your estate after you subtract the specific and general bequests.

Individual ownership – Means that you alone own and control the entire interest in a piece of property.

Joint ownership – Means that you along with one or more other people own a piece of property (cash, stocks, land, etc.).

Joint Tenants with right of survivorship – In the case your spouse automatically inherits your share (in stocks and such), regardless of what your will says.

Beneficiary designations – Help control the disposition of property upon death, is another way of passing property "outside of the will." Most commonly found in retirement plans and life insurance policies.

Dying intestate – Mean dying without a will, which can cause complications that vary from state to state.

Guardian of the state – The person designated to manage the assets for your minor children, until they become adults (age 18).

Guardian of the person – This person or persons will be in charge of raising your children. They make decisions on your children's education, religious training, upbringing and so forth. They become the substitute for you!

Final Comments on Wills

- If you are married and have children, it is good planning to have your wills drawn up at the same time. They are called interlocking or reciprocal wills. The wills are written to meet the objectives of both parents. These wills will usually name the caretakers of their children should both parents die at the same time.
- Your survivors must pay federal taxes if your taxable estate (equal to your gross estate minus debts and expenses) exceeds $1,500,000 (rising to as high as $3.5 Million in 2009).
- Plan your estate by percentages, not by fixed dollar figures, because your assets can increase or decrease before you die.
- Consider trusts as a way of passing on your property especially if you have a large estate or if children are your successors.
- As you grow older plan on making periodic changes every 5 to 10 years, updating additional children, executor and guardian changes, divorce, newly accumulated assets such as cars, real estate or other property.

Be Aware of Probate

If you die without a will, Probate is the legal procedure that mandates how your estate will be distributed. Under the normal process of having a will your executor must file your will with probate court when you die, then they determine if the will is valid or not. Once that obstacle is passed your assets are distributed. But when you don't have a will, probate court and the state guidelines you live in takes over. The probate process can take months to work through and may cost as much as 10% of the assets of your estate. Wills that enter probate are public documents, which means anyone can find out about your financial affairs and how much money you left behind. Remember that money tied up in pension plans, IRAs, Keoghs, Totten Trust bank accounts, and life insurance plans pass directly to your named beneficiary. Jointly held property (such as your home, cars, lake house, motorcycles, etc.) usually glides beyond probate's eyes. In most states, they also have a simplified version of probate for assets that total less than $40,000 to $50,000. This type of probate is called a small estate proceeding, and is much less complex and costly than a regular probate. And assets held in a living trust pass to named beneficiaries without going through the probate procedures.

Power of Attorney

The importance of a drafted document for the Durable Power of Attorney cannot be over emphasized. The Power of Attorney allows you to appoint someone else to handle your affairs in your place should you become unable to do so yourself. As young adults this is a document you can set up quite easily by purchasing a will software package or contact an attorney to have this Power of Attorney document created. I recommend combining the financial powers with the medical powers in the same Durable Power of Attorney document. On the medical side, in response to the Christine Busalacchi and Nancy Cruzan cases, the Missouri legislature revised the statutes in order to permit the holder of a Durable Power of Attorney for Health Care to make the decision to either withdraw or prohibit life support, and even to withhold or withdraw water and food by tube feeding. Therefore choose this person carefully, and if you are married the obvious person is your spouse. I highly recommend you institute a Power of Attorney document!

Trusts

A trust is another form of property ownership that is used in estate planning. A trust is a legal arrangement that enables an individual, called a **grantor** or **settlor**, to give property to another person or group of other people to hold for a specific reason or person. The assets are under the control of a **trustee**, who manages and distributes the assets written out by the grantor. Trusts provide a lot of flexibility in planning to manage your estate taxes and passing property to your heirs. All trusts, no matter how they function, are either **living trusts** (taking effect during your lifetime) or **testamentary trusts** (taking effect only after your die).

There are two basic types of trusts:

1. **Irrevocable Trust** – Meaning that you can't revoke, amend, modify, or change the trust.

2. **Revocable Trust** – Meaning it can be revoked, modified, or amended. Revocable trusts are much more common than irrevocable trusts.

Every trust is made up of three partners. The *trustor* (*grantor* or *settlor*) is the person whose assets are placed in the trust. The *trustee* is the person who manages the property you have in the trust. This person could be the same person as the *trustor*, or it could be a close friend or relative, someone you trust and has some financial expertise. Or choose a professional such as an accountant or an attorney, or an institution like a bank or a brokerage firm. The third party is the *beneficiary*, the person who receives the benefits of the trust, whether income or principal. A trust is a formal written document, which you can write yourself via help from books or software packages. Don't forget to show the documents to a lawyer for review, and don't waste any time with questions or mistakes **YOU** might make on your own.

Living Trusts

The most common technique used to avoid probate court is to set up a living trust, also known as a *"revocable inter vivos trust."* It allows you to place assets into a trust while you live. Whatever property you transfer to the trust is no longer owned by you, instead it's owned by the trust, which is a separate legal entity from you. You can even set up the trust to continue after you die, having it run by your co-trustee or successor trustee. Only property that is not in the living trust at the date of your death can be probated. Thus if you have transferred all of your assets to the trust prior to your death, you own no assets to probate court at your death.

Advantages of a Revocable Living Will Trust:
- Avoids probate court.
- Flexibility in that it can be designed for income and inheritance.
- A Trust is far less subject to court contest or challenge.
- Allows for a quicker payment of inheritance to beneficiaries.
- Ability to change provisions as often as desired.
- Maintains privacy and better security for your personal financial affairs.

- Allows you to control your assets after death of a spouse.
- Great savings in administrative and Probate costs and expenses.

Disadvantages of a Revocable Living Will Trust:
- Must transfer your assets to the Living Trust.
- Typically costs more than setting up a will.
- Makes refinancing of real estate more challenging.
- Probate provides a short statue of limitations in some states. In Missouri, the statute is the same length of time if appropriate notice is given.

The Disclaimer Type Living Trust

In this type of trust, you are still trying to ensure that the estate tax credit can be used for the death of the first spouse, but it allows the survivor much more flexibility in the extent and nature of the credit shelter funding. A properly drafted Disclaimer Living Trust allows married couples and their families to protect at least $3.0 million on estate taxes. To start with, every person gets a $1,500,000 exemption from estate taxes (which is part of the Unified Tax Credit). If you are married, you qualify for the unlimited marital deductions. There is no taxation on the estate upon the death of the first spouse, and when the second spouse dies everything over $1,500,000 is subject to estate taxes. The amount of the estate tax credit is subject to much change in the coming years, with the credit reaching as high as $2.5 million in 2009. The estate tax repeal in 2010 and it's reinstation in 2011 brings it back to the 2001 number of $1,000,000.

Other Types of Trusts

Grantor-Retained Interest Trusts (GRITs). They deal with securities or real estate, and are used to help relatives or friends benefit from your estate.

Support Trusts. These trusts are used to provide your spouse and children income, to support their accustomed lifestyle, especially if you were the sole income earner.

Charitable Remainder Unit Trusts (CRUT). This trust enables you to bequeath your assets to a charity, while at the same time allows you to take a tax deduction on the property's value. You can also receive payment on the value of the donated assets.

Charitable Lead Trusts. With this trust, you donate assets to your favorite charitable institution, such as from the sale of a stock, to a qualified charity. During your lifetime you also receive an annuity generated by the trust assets. When you die, the charity retains the assets.

Q-TIP Trusts. This Qualified Terminal Interest Property trust is used mainly by wealthy people. It lets you pass on an unlimited amount of money to your spouse without your estate taking a tax charge. Someone other than your wife is the appointed trustee. Neither the wife nor anyone else can give the money away. The IRS watches carefully how funds are dispersed in this type of trust.

Insurance Trusts. These are life insurance trusts, which are irrevocable. They provide so that the death benefit from your life insurance policy does not transfer into your estate, which could add to the estate's value beyond the lifetime estate tax exemption, and thus create estate taxes.

Resources for More Information

Life Insurance has an **Insurance Company Yellow Pages**, which provides a directory of web sites for individual life insurance companies. (lifecom.com)

On Health Insurance the **National Committee for Quality Assurance (NCQA)** allows you to look at quality ratings it has given to HMOs. (hiaa.org)

Council for Affordable Health Insurance (CAHI) will provide information on a variety of health insurance topics and is a good resource on Medical Savings Accounts. (cahi.com)

Insurance News Network has good information about the basics of homeowner's, auto and life insurance. (insure.com)

The Insurance Information Institute (III) is a good source to look at for information on property and casualty, along with health and life insurance. (iii.org)

For individual disability insurance look at the **American Association of Individual Investors**. (aaii.com) 800-428-2244

To get information on rating services that share the financial health of an insurance company contact these rating service sites:

A. M. Best	(ambest.com)
Moody's Investor Service	(moodys.com)
Duff & Phelps Credit Rating	(dufflc.com)

Questions on Insurance in your state contact:

Missouri State Insurance Department, 301 West High Street, 6 North, Jefferson City, MO 65102, 573-751-4126.

Illinois State Insurance Department, 320 West Washington Street, 4th floor, Springfield, IL, 60601, 217-785-0116.

For Life Insurance these web sites can help:

TermQuote	(rcinet.com/-termquote)	800-444-8376
InsuranceQuote	(iquote.com)	800-972-1104
Selectquote	(selectquote.com)	800-289-5807
MasterQuote	(masterquote.com)	800-627-5433

For help on financing cars or homes and rates on credit cards:

(financenter.com)

(elibrary.com/intuit/-define what you want to search for)

Recommended books include:

How to Buy a New Car, by Consumer Reports Books, 1-800-500-9760.

Insurance for Dummies, by Jack Hungemann, Wiley Publishing.

References:

(Insurance.com)	(farmers.com)
(iii.org)	(naic.org)
(insure.com)	(highwaysafety.org)
(statefarm.com)	(mief.org)
(allstate.com)	(aaii.com)

8

INCOME DIVERSIFICATION

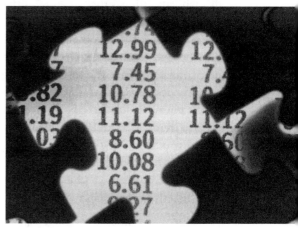

This last chapter is designed to make your creative juices flow. Income diversification in this context means **"YOU"** viewing different alternatives to making money aside from your day job. Not everyone will expand their horizons on this concept of raising your talent levels to higher degrees. What if...you are a talented musician, but teaching music in a public school system isn't your passion or patience. Let's say for example you decide to attend a technical school, become an HVAC specialist and make a decent living. But on the weekends you get involved playing in a rock'n tight jamm'n band. Taking that extra money you earn, invest for your future financial planning or use that income to save towards a down payment on a house. I want to instill in all of you that there are many hours outside of your day job. Develop hobbies or interests geared to your enjoyment; use that as a diversion from your 8-5 job. Rather than spending needless, wasted hours in front of a TV or computer most evenings, invest some of your time in something worthwhile that down the road can pay financial rewards. My wife over the years has developed a hobby in gardening and landscaping. By day she works as a dental hygienist earning great money and on some evenings and weekends for her get away time she designs and plants masterfully crafted flowers, hostas, and shrubbery displays in our yard. It relieves tension; she can spend an hour or multiple hours and carefully details a mix of colors, smells and ornate flowers and tree shrubs. She has monthly magazine subscriptions to get ideas and over the winter months she plots her garden growth for the next spring season. Down the road she would like to take horticulture classes at the Botanical Garden and someday market her skills with a nursery or landscape company.

What if...just be creative and think outside the box! Make a list of diversification ideas that fit you...as the individual person you are. Define, critique, and modify your lifestyle as you age. Develop a hobby, a talent, a passion that you enjoy. Start a collection of coins and stamps, develop that collection for 30 plus years and when you turn sixty sell that collection. Take the money and run. You might run to buy a new car (you deserve it); you might buy that cabin on a lake in Minnesota you've always desired to have, or simply invest the money to cushion your retirement. And you will thank me, for starting the planning that netted you $100,000 or $250,000. It's never too late to expand your free hours to make them pay you great dividends down the road of life. I call it "cruisin'" and not "losin'", you're investing extra hours to reap benefits in your later years. In the following pages we will look at some avenues for income diversification including: hobbies, crafts, collections, rental properties, land speculation, sports memorabilia, and buying things that over time increase in dollar value. My purpose here is to get you to develop your interest and talents to help benefit your success levels in your life and diversify your income for your future years.

Free hours viewing TV and surfing the Internet are TIME ROBBERS = Stolen Time!

Free hours spent with hobby/collection/side business = HIGHER SUCCESS RATIO!

What About That Hobby?

When you get home from a long day at work, instead of turning on the TV, I want you to turn on your creative juices and talents. Heh, you can still have your TV time, but after you finish dinner maybe play ball with the kids or take an hour to work on your hobby. I recommend you develop a hobby that fits your style, make it something you love to do. For the pure enjoyment of pleasing yourself, pour your heart, mind and soul into the effort and it will pay many rewards as you grow older. I encourage you to talk to friends, neighbors, co-workers, maybe your parents and ask them what hobbies they have and why they have them.

Webster's Dictionary defines *hobby* as "a pursuit outside one's regular occupation engaged in especially for relaxation."

Let's take a look at some hobbies you might acquire a taste for:

-Backpacking/hiking/camping
-Bicycle touring
-Building bird houses
-Cooking & baking
-Furniture making
-Home audio
-Hunting
-Model airplanes/cars
-Traveling

-Beer making
-Bird watching
-Building doll houses
-Fishing
-Gardening
-Home video
-Landscaping
-Solving crossword puzzles
-Wood working

Getting into Crafts

Making crafts is fun and can be very creative. Craft making has been around for centuries. The Indians made baskets for collecting food and pottery vessels for carrying water. Colonial women used their old worn out clothing, cutting up patches and making quilts to keep warm. Early explorers and hunters not only ate the meat of the animal they killed, but crafted deer and buffalo hides into jackets, vests, blankets, shoes, and carrying packs. All these early "crafted" items became cherished American Folk art that is now housed in our museums at the Gateway Arch and Natural History Museum.

Crafting is a great way to release your creative talents and pass leisure time at home. As an added feature you can turn certain craft hobbies into moneymaking endeavors. There are craft fairs, exhibitions, shows held all over the state of Missouri. Attending craft shows will expose you to travel, new friends and craft comrades, along with viewing other ideas your fellow crafters have generated. The rewards of crafting can include:

• A way to relax and unwind (way to fight stress).
• The pride and joy of self-accomplishment and fulfillment in creating something.
• Constantly creating new ideas for simple made projects.
• A way to save money and a way to make money.
• Decorate your home with crafts.

- An inexpensive way to be a great giver of gifts.
- Possibly find a new career path through crafting.
- Teaching crafts to others can be a rewarding experience.
- Build a tradition of sharing your craft knowledge with your children & grandchildren.

Let's take a look at some craft categories:

-Appliqué	-Baskets	-Bead necklaces
-Candle making	-Crochet	-Cross-stitch
-Decoupage	-Faux Finishing	-Glass blowing
-Holiday crafts	-Jewelry making	-Nature crafting
-Needle point	-Paint crafts	-Patchworking
-Pottery	-Quilting	-Rubber-stamping -Saw
murals	-Scrap booking	-Sewing
-Soap making	-Specialty wrapping	-Stained glass
-Stenciling	-Tye-dying	-Wreaths

Craft magazines include:

Crafts 'n Things	Martha Stewart Living
Memory Makers	Family Circle
The Stitchery Magazine	Weekend Crafts
Kid's Crafts	Sew News

Establishing a Collection

I believe over time we all become collectors. I inherited my father's hunting paraphernalia. A couple of his shotguns, deer rifle, a 410 double barrel shotgun, knee high laced hunting boots, a jacket with 20 pockets and various gun cleaning supplies. Over the years my wife has called me a junk collector. I just collect junk, thinking "I can't throw that away, I might use it someday." But realistically, collecting has grown to huge proportions. It's not a fad, it's collection mania, and it can be an obsession for some people. More and more people are turning to collecting "something" and enjoying the ride. There is some money to be made if you have what the other person is looking for. Remember in 1998 when Mark McGwire's seventieth home-run baseball sold for $3 million? Todd McFarlane, a Comic book writer who loves baseball, bought it as a collector's item. Incredible! Did you know that original Barbie dolls can cost as much as $5,000? My GI

Joe doll would probably bring in some money if I could ever find him. Yea, I had a GI Joe when I was a kid 40 plus years ago.

Collecting has always been a driving force, more so for the rich and noble. The great art collections of kings in Egypt, the Chinese Dynasties have so much rich history in their temples, fortresses, castles, and museums that are loaded with hand painted artwork, ancient costumes, golden idols, and swords of the Samurai – all of these are collectibles!   The great Pharaohs thought they could take their priceless treasures with them to the next world, so their tombs were full of jewelry, gold, silver, diamonds, pottery, paintings and clothes. The Catholic Church has a very large collection of paintings of the masters. History is rich with different cultures that consummate vast collections of wealth for many different nations and countries, all preserved in museums for the entire world to see.

Webster's dictionary defines *collection*, "the act or process of collecting, an accumulation of objects gathered for study, comparison, or exhibition or as a hobby."

My advice is that you begin to accumulate a collection that you can enjoy and have fun collecting over the next 30 to 40 years of your life. It will consume some of your free time, give you a defined purpose to do some research, travel, investigate and motivate you as a collector. Then as you draw near retirement find a buyer and sell all or a portion of your collection to have extra money in your treasure chest for your golden years. I have a quick story to share about my son Blake. I have 3 daughters and one son, so when ever we would go on vacation or a weekend trip – what do you think the girls enjoyed doing the most? Shopping and more shopping, and window-shopping more. I would take Blake and we headed off to search for pawnshops, trinket stores and the like as we started a pocketknife collection for Blake when he was about 6 years old. It was a great father and son time to go searching for pocketknives while the rest of the troops did their "girl-time" shopping episodes. Over the years we had a lot of fun and now Blake has a collection of over 35 pocketknives from all over the country.

As a collector here are some important keys to be aware of:

- **Collection item functionality** – An item (collectable) starts out as a thing, it is valued only for its pure function. The item then builds interest, and becomes a desirable, which can create a supply vs. demand principle that drives the value of the item higher. And last of all the item becomes a collectible, or maybe an antique, and now people want to have it in their possession for its appearance and value, not its function.

- **Price** – How much an item costs is a key factor to whether it will become a collectible. The desirables start off being affordable and available to collectors. Over time the collectibles become fewer and are more expensive, finally the fewest collectibles are extremely costly.

- **Quantity** – How many of a certain collectible helps determine the value of that item. If there are many of that item it will rarely become a collectible, but the fewer the market has to offer, interest sparks and suddenly it becomes a collectible.

- **Perceived beauty** – What one person sees in a collectible can be totally different from another person. Collectors become engrossed with their collection, they enjoy the research, the hunt, the touch and feel of their collectible, and how well it is crafted. The color, shape, design, and size of their collection is what turns them on.

- **Condition** – The better the quality level (condition) of an antique or collectible, the more value it will have. Preserve and protect the condition of your collection in the best way possible. Example: Keep stamp books flat, keep coins in protective plastic cases, and don't put antique furniture to busy use.

- **Historical links** – Many collectors feel a passion about the past. The item they collect reminds them of something from their past, a simpler and slower paced era. People who collect Beatles or Elvis Presley memorabilia have memories of the wild 1960's. Keep in mind the more that pop cultural items preserve the feelings of the past, the more probable they will become collectibles.

- **Present day links** – Some collectors they like the appeal of past and present. For example, their collection might be toy wagons. They collect antique toy wagons and also include toy wagons purchased today. Their collection is still being created in a similar form but the changes of craftsmanship, color, make and model is most appealing. They are not tied only to a historical past but have a link to modern day lifestyle.

Terms to be familiar with as a collector include:

Desirable – A desirable is a collected object whose value is uncertain. Desirables can include Star War figures, Chatty Cathy dolls, and pokemon cards for example.

Collectible – A collectible is a desired (coveted) item made in the last 50 years. Collectibles include comic books, matchsafes, or Barbie dolls for example.

Antiques – An antique must be at least 100 years old, but most dealers and collectors consider 75 to 100 years to be an acceptable range to rank as an "antique." Antiques include vintage crystal, china, silver, and furniture for example.

Dealer – This person is interested in buying, selling and trading, usually to make a profit. They usually have a shop, storefront or building where they do their dealing from. They attend monthly auctions, fairs, swap-meets to buy and sell items. They usually are very knowledgeable about the items they purchase, buying what they can afford for the best dollar value, and sometimes keeping the best for themselves.

Collector – This person is passionate and emotional with the items they collect. They possess a collection because they like (love) the item and consider their collection as cherished children. They receive pleasure from their collection and frown upon selling their prized items for any amount of money. They may or may not be interested in buying, selling, or trading.

Investor – They buy an item with premeditation of reselling it at a profit. They get pure excitement at the thought of the profit winnings vs. possessing the item. They enjoy buying, selling and trading, but consider items in their collection to be merchandise. They are business people first, collectors second.

Appraiser – When you need an expert opinion on specific collectors item contact an appraiser. Not knowing the full value of an authentic collectible can affect your dollar spending when you plan to buy or sell a collectible. You can contact the Appraiser Association of America (AAA) for a referral of an appraiser in your area. Contact them at (appaisersassoc.org). You might also consult with the American Society of Appraisers, contact them at (appraisers.org).

Let's take a look at some collection categories:

-Advertising Items
-Antique Tools
-Art Prints
-Baseballs (Autographed)
-Baseball Cards
-Beatles Memorabilia
-Bottle Caps
-Christmas Ornaments
-Civil War Equipment
-Coin Operated Machines
-Costumes
-Dolls
-Folk Art
-Gas Pumps
-Hat Pins
-Jukeboxes
-Knives
-Marbles
-Menus
-Minerals
-Magnets
-Olympic Memorabilia
-Paperweights
-Playing Cards
-Pulp Magazines
-Quilts (old & handmade)
-Rock n' Roll Memorabilia
-Sea Shells
-Soda Cans (vintage)
-Teddy Bears
-Theater Items
-Tools
-Walt Disney Items

-Antique Clothing
-Antique Furniture
-Ashtrays
-Barbershop Items
-Beanie Babies
-Beer
-Boy Scout Memorabilia
-Circus Memorabilia
-Coca Cola Memorabilia
-Comic Books
-Country Store Items
-Elvis Presley Memorabiliam
-Fishing Lures
-Glassware
-Jazz Memorabilia
-Keys (old ones)
-License Plates
-Matchbooks
-Military Items
-Movie Memorabilia
-Norman Rockwell Memorabilia
-Paintings
-Photographs
-Plates
-Pottery
-Rackets
-Rubber stamps
-Sheet Music
-Stoneware
-Trunks
-Thimbles
-Toys
-Wine

-Arrowheads
-Art Glass
-Autographs
-Banks
-Baskets
-Beer Cans
-Cameras
-Clocks
-Coins
-Corkscrews
-Dinnerware
-Foreign Money
-Hollywood Memorabilia
-Jewelry
-Kitchen Utensils
-Locks (antique)
-Medals
-Model Railroad Items
-Music Boxes
-Paper Money
-Pinups
-Political Items
-Postcards
-Railroad Memorabilia
-Schoolhouse Items
-Silver Items
-Sports Memorabilia
-Telephones
-Tobacco Item
-Trading Cards

I asked an acquaintance of mine, Peter Rexford, who is a nation-ally syndicated columnist whose column appears in dozens of papers around the United States, including the St. Louis Post Dispatch, to offer his thoughts on philatelic and numismatic collecting/investing:

What's rarely covered in the mainstream media is the enduring interest and investment in tangible assets. Tops on the list of collectible assets that have a record of long-term increasing value are rare coins, stamps, postal history and currency.

The intrinsic fascination with collectibles such as these stem from the allure of their engraving, sculptural skill as well as the fact that they do, or once had, actual value as legal tender or as government issued specie.

The simple truth concerning any tangible investment is that value is created by 1) Rarity and 2) Sustained demand. You must have both for the collectible to maintain or increase in value.

For well over a century, rare coins, stamps and related collectibles have drawn the interest and dollars of ardent collectors. Today, buyers in-clude casual and serious collectors as well as art aficionados industrialists, celebrities, sports stars and others who have come into money. The reason? They appreciate the beauty of the collectible, enjoy owning something that's recognized as rare and want to diversify their holdings into non-traditional areas that have proven potential for long-term profits.

Naturally, beginning investors can't expect to purchase a rare $20 gold piece or a set of classic stamps for, say $25,000. And, truth be told, that can be all for the better. Just as it's inadvisable to put all your money in one stock, so too is it for tangible investments.

Rather, by beginning slowly, purchasing what you can afford, and gaining knowledge about potential future purchases along the way will allow you to assemble a solid portfolio of collectibles. As has been proven time and time again, small purchases bought and held over time can easily grow into holdings of significant value.

As with any investment, knowledge is power. The more you know, the more you'll make. The great part about collectibles is that garnering the knowledge about the items – their history, lore, pedigree or legacy – is far more fun than sifting through annual reports trying to make heads or tails out of endless financial ledgers.

Affordable memberships in national organizations such as the Ameri-can Numismatic Association (ANA) or American Philatelic Society

(APS) will reward you many times over through their insightful publications with information on grading, pricing and trends. The same is true for attending a few major expositions or conventions. In short order, you'll find yourself gaining the knowledge and confidence to make your first, second and subsequent purchases. As your collection grows in numbers and in value, so will your enjoyment!
Source: Peter Rexford, Nationally Syndicated Columnist.

Sports Collectibles

If you like sports, or are an athlete and like to compete in sports and games, then a sports collection could be a great category area to choose. Because of the popularity of college and professional sports, sports collectibles have become a growing and profitable business. The field has a wide range from collecting trading cards to autographs of key athletic stars. As with any collection, rarity and condition of the item are key factors to determining the object's value. If you can find a trading card signed by that athlete, it is more valuable than his card without the signature. If you want to get your children interested in collectibles, sports collections are a great place to start.

Sports collections might include:

-Autographs of sports stars   -Baseballs
-Baseball bats   -Baseball gloves
-Bowling pins   -College banners
-Footballs   -Football helmets
-Golf balls   -Golf caddie bags
-Golf clubs   -Sports jerseys
-Sports memorabilia   -Trading cards
-Uniforms

Recommended sports magazines include:

Baseball Cards
Sports Collectors Digest
Baseball Hobby News

Diversifying with Rental Properties

For the past 20 years I have been involved with acquiring and securing rental properties. My older brother (25 years my senior) had many years of experience and was very influential in guiding my first steps into the purchase of rental houses. There are plenty of resources at your local bookstore and library on how to buy and sell rental properties. My experience comes from the purchase of single-family homes so I shall share that side. My wife Kristine and I decided early in our first year of marriage that we wanted to collect rental properties. I contacted my brother who had been in the business for over 15 years for help on getting started. He advised us on laying out a plan on how to build up some equity first in our house. You will, down the road as you get started, certainly need some capital (money) to build your business. We learned to view our rental properties as a separate business entity, knowing the extra hours invested were apart from our day jobs. It can be a lot of work, but it can also be a great way to build equity in real estate, which in most cases has appreciated versus depreciated.

I was fortunate to collect a portion of my inheritance money early from my mother, soon after my father passed away when I was 24 years old. I had set some goals at the time to leave my band director position in Adrian, MO (located near Kansas City) and move back home to St. Louis and establish my roots there. I was ready to settle down, buy my first starter home and for the first time in my life put the word "marriage" into my vocabulary. Things happened quickly for me in the summer of 1979. I met my future wife at the Strassenfest downtown, asking her to polka with me; I got a date that night with Kris. Four weeks later I was seeing stars with this girl and I asked her to marry me. During the fast courtship I had been house hunting and put a contract on a bungalow in Webster Groves. We were married November 17, 1979 and moved into our honeymoon haven. I used the $10,000 inheritance from my mother to purchase the house, which costs $35,000. Kris and I set goals together as husband and wife, one being that we wanted to wait to start a family at least four years. We had agreed on collecting rental properties and we determined in our game plan (with help from relatives) to put our extra money into extra principal payments on our home mortgage loan. For three plus years we did this. We started our family in the fifth year; staying one more year in our Webster home and then purchased our second house with an FHA loan. To achieve our capital spending money, we took a second mortgage (line of credit) on the Webster Groves house. After 6 and a half years the house had increased in value to just under $55,000. We were able to get up to 75% money funding and thus established a $40,000 line of credit (second mortgage) to start collecting rental properties.

Buying a house with an FHA loan is always a good option. You usually are required to put a down payment of 3%. The second house purchase was a row house in Dogtown. I negotiated the price down from $47,500 to $40,000 after a number of counter offers. The owners were an older couple retiring to Florida, they had their house being built down there, I put the contract offers to them in December and they accepted because their house was finishing in April. The deal ended up with my closing on the house in January, they lived in the house paying me rent for 2 months, then we moved in that April. With their upfront rent money included in closing costs, my total out of pocket money was $1,300 to purchase the house. We lived in that house for 2 years, meanwhile I purchased another large 3-story house in St. Louis, near Maplewood. I bought that house for $40,000 with a $10,000 down payment. It needed some work, two college buddies had purchased the house living in it and rehabbing to about 80% and then they hit burn out and were ready to sell. I ended up spending one entire summer working every weeknight and most weekends over at the Commonwealth house finishing the work. I learned a lot of carpentry, plumbing and restoring wood floors in that time. We moved in that house in May of 1989, living there only 6 months before I came across another deal on a house in Maryland Heights that I could not pass up. This house took my family from city schools to Parkway School district and a solid move to St. Louis County, which was on our goal list. The best way to buy a single family or duplex is to plan to live in the house yourself, for at least for 6 to 12 months as an owner occupied tenant. The interest rates are better and usually the financing terms become more workable than non-owner occupied rental property.

My brother helped me with creative financing on the McKelvey house. Again I found a motivated seller, who was building a new house in Chesterfield and needed to sell this house to complete the deal on his next house. The owner wanted $92,000 for the house; I only wanted to spend around $12,000 or so for my total down payment. The financing with banks at the time were requiring 20% down payment, I made an offer for $82,000 on the house, but in my proposal stated that we put the sales price at $92,000, and he would give me $10,000 in cash 5 days prior to closing. I found favor with the man, he was desperate to close on the house and he decided to take my offer. With his $10,000 cash toward my $18,400 (20% down payment) I had the money I wanted to spend, including what I needed for closing cost. We ended up living in that house ten years, before moving to the house we currently reside in.

My Tips for Rental Properties

1. Spend your time carefully deciding where you want to purchase rental properties, remember that location is so very important in real estate. Once you determine the area, drive the neighborhoods on your lunch hour, evenings after work or on the weekends searching the "for sale" signs. Call real estate agents in that area to help you maintain a print out of "for sale" listings in the location you choose. **Remember**: Location, location, location!

2. Put in a lower conservative bid on the house and see what the seller counters in their offer. Always strive to find a motivated seller, someone who is desperate to sell for some urgent reason or another. You can get better deals this way.

3. Look for properties that have solid substance in all areas such as age of roof, foundation, windows, plumbing, electrical wiring, insulation, yard appearance, overall general good check points everywhere. Confer with your real estate agent on their opinion of the house, study and read books to know what areas you can repair, making adjustments in your counter offers on the final purchase price.

4. Keep things simple when you can, especially if you have more than one rental property. Buy 5-gallon buckets of paint, either white or beige, and use the same paint in all your houses. Don't worry about curtains or drapes, just deal with shades or blinds on the windows. If you have decent wood floors polyurethane them and pass on carpet. If you do use carpet in rental houses, I have tried to use the same carpet company (Edwards Carpet) to draw upon them for special discounts for buying carpet from them over the years.

5. Look carefully at the exterior of the house; you want siding all ready on the house if you can find it. Walk the yard and look at the age of the trees. I have taken down some rather large trees at rental properties, the ones that were too big, like in Webster Groves, I have had to pay significantly to have them professionally taken down. So be very aware of outside maintenance, including bushes, shrubs and tree limbs that you as the landlord are responsible for. The tenant will cut the grass but other yard maintenance the landlord will be upkeeping.

6. Don't be afraid to tackle an update or remodel to a kitchen or bathroom. There is information in books at the library, on the Internet and the experts at Lowe's and Home Depot can explain how to lay tile, flooring, tiling and grouting to bathroom walls. Learning to do it yourself is part of stepping into the rental property business. I have learned a lot over the years and I have enjoyed the process along with the satisfaction and pride in all my projects.

7. I ended up buying two of my rental properties on busy streets (Laclede Station Road and McKelvey Road). My advertising to rent the houses has always been easier because I simply put up my "For Rent" sign in the yard; it generates many phone inquiries, which rent the house easier and quicker.

8. Don't be afraid to advertise in the local community paper, The Journal, or the Post-Dispatch. Over the years I have also found companies that you can call and they post houses for rent on their call inquiry list. I have also printed up my own "House for Rent" notices, identifying the rent amount, location, bedrooms, baths, washer/dryer, etc...then on my lunch hour or after work I would run these handouts to the local laundromat, pub & grills, restaurants, hardware stores, grocery stores and anywhere else I could post my flier.

9. Type up your own rental application on your computer. When screening applicants, I meet them at the property to show the house, also have hosted open houses from two to four in the afternoon on Saturday and Sundays. Make sure on the application you include driver's license and social security numbers (these two can be used to check credit and with law enforcement), yearly income, supervisors name and number where they work, past landlords

names and numbers, current address and current landlord. I also require at least 5 to 7 character references, list their name, relationship and phone number. I call every one of them, asking all kinds of questions and taking notes.

10. Almost every time you re-rent the house plan on painting almost every room in the house, or at least doing some major touch up work. I replace all burned out lightbulbs (and there are many), make sure to clean the house spotless, including the bathroom. While the house is vacant for a day or so I also spray for bugs, insects, ants, rodents inside and outside. Yes, you too can become a bug spray person once you become a landlord.

11. In my leases I do a couple of things different. I tell all my tenants up front I will come by beginning of each month to collect cash or cashier check for rent. I write in the lease that I will do a 5 to 10 minute walk through inspection of the house each month to check on things like water faucets, sink drains and furnace filters. This way I see the house each month and the tenant sees me, they can let me know if there are any problems that keeps open communication levels with your tenants.

12. I make my tenants responsible for paying all the utilities (I give them a list of the utility companies to call to have their names changed for that property upon moving in). They also have to cut the grass or hire someone to maintenance it. I trim bushes and trees in the fall or spring and I don't suggest planting flowers or hostas or nice things, most tenants rarely do much more then cut the grass.

13. I collect a last month's rent in cash when I sign a lease form. Then when they move in on the first of the month I collect cash rent payment for that month. I hold their deposit money for 3 to 4 weeks upon vacancy, checking with utility companies on overdue bills, and depending upon how they leave the property, mail the appropriate deposit to them at their current next residence.

14. Consider buying a FIZZBO, which are sellers who aren't using brokers or real estate agents. Basically, a **FSBO** is a "For Sale By Owner" property. They are looking to save 6 to 7% agent/broker commissions and have the house priced at a better bargain price. The longer the house sits on the market, the better the opportunity you have to buy the house at a lower asking price.

15. Shop for houses in the off-season. Peak season for selling homes is spring, fall and summer. Purchasing a home in the middle of winter or right after Thanksgiving and Christmas can sometimes help you buy a lot cheaper.

16. Buy smaller houses for rental, I am thinking Cape Cod, Colonial, Ranch, Tudor or Split- level. Smaller houses cost less, are easier to maintain and can have better variables with monthly rental fees.

17. I try to and have been successful renting my houses with "NO Pets." I have a big worded area at the top of the lease application stating no pets, but if the tenant checks out great on their references and I believe they will make a solid renter I have looked at small dogs or cats. They are charged an additional Pet deposit of $300 to $500.

18. My advice is find a good accountant once you get started in rental properties. Real estate rules tend to change slightly each year and your accountant will know how they affect your depreciation and appreciation with rentals. Let the expert do their job in preparing your tax returns, in a correct manner, so that the IRS doesn't come knocking on your door.

19. Take time to learn about the tax shelters that rental properties can afford you. You can write off a lot of areas such as car mileage, maintenance needs, hiring your kids at reasonable hourly rates, depreciation, etc., which all tie in to lowering your taxable income.

20. My best advice in real estate is to start out buying single-family homes. They usually appreciate well in value, the financing can be obtained by both a lower interest rate and a higher loan-to-value, and single-family homes are the most liquid of real estate investments.

Other means of buying or locating property might include:

- Real estate agents/brokers, friends or neighbors.
- Driving neighborhoods looking for "FSBO" signs.
- Read classified ads, both "For Sale" and "For Lease."
- Advertise in paper for property to buy for rental use.
- Go to county courthouse to check on public records for eviction notices (call the owner of the property to relieve his headache) or divorce records (spouses going through a divorce are often eager to sell the house quickly for splitting the cash).

- Network with real estate agents and mortgage loan officers who might have leads on houses for sale or foreclosure.
- Buy legal newspaper or check the courthouse records for Probate records. Heirs who recently inherited property might not want the hassle; they desire the cash, especially if they live out of state.
- Look at foreclosures, take the time to learn and study how they work. Check courthouse bulletin boards and records as well as learn the process. Two good web sites are (foreclosure.com) and (foreclosurefreesearch.com).

Recommended books include:

Real Estate Investing from A to Z, by William H. Pivar, McGraw-Hill

Landlording & Property Management, by Mark Weiss & Dan Baldwin, Adams Media Corp

Speculative Land Buying

I briefly mention this area just to make you aware of purchasing land on speculation for investment purposes. My wife and I back in the early eighties bought a lot of wooded land at Raintree Plantation, a lake development community in Hillsboro, Missouri. We paid $6,500 for a ¼ acre lot, which included full country club membership. We did access the lake, the swimming pool; I played golf a couple times in the summer and ate at the restaurant over the first 5 years. As we grew older and our family developed with young kids we eventually used the accommodations less often. Until recently when we sold the lot for a $2,000 loss did I feel better having been released from that property. We bought the lot thinking the land everywhere would develop and hoped in 15 years to sell the property. We made a wrong decision in lot placement, were not able to sell the land for a profit. The community at Raintree did prosper and develop nicely over the years, but if we had bought a lot adjoining the lakefront we would have made a profit. So careful selection of land, its location and speculation to how that area will benefit you down the road is very risky. I couldn't rent the lot to someone, we paid taxes and membership dues over the years, once the property was paid off, they continued to suck up our money. And keep in mind; we borrowed money with a small down payment, paying interest on the three-year loan.

But there are valuable land buying opportunities to look for. I had a friend who purchased a 3 acre lot in a new subdivision going in at Wildwood, he bought there simply at the very beginning of the development, holding on to the tract of land and selling in five years later when the subdivision had developed completely and was able to make a $30,000 profit, minus his loan borrowing, closing and interest charges and taxes on the land.

If you can estimate huge growth market trends with housing expansion and business development and have the cash flow to back up the mortgage and tax payments then carefully plot where you think purchasing speculative land will pay off in the future years. Factors such as price of the land, local zoning, direction of interest rates, environmental regulations, and the current trends in the economy can all have an effect on your purchase. The boom in housing and business development in St. Charles, St. Peters, O'Fallon and Wentzville has been substantial. I am sure that speculators in the 1980's who bought land in Wentzville and who were able to hold on a number of years have benefited financially. But please be aware that land speculation is risky, you need inside knowledge, understanding of the investment criteria and a lot of luck to cushion any unforeseen problems that will hinder financial success.

Of course buying land way out in the country to hunt or fish on the property is a different endeavor. Usually rural areas are the best place to buy up to twenty to forty acres of woodland for pure love of hunting. Talk to other hunters, talk to farmers who own land in the area you want to hunt and sometimes they can be your best means of buying land for sale by owner, versus going through a real estate agent in that county.

Investing Your Talents and Interest in Sports Cars

One area you might consider, especially if you like cars, and even better if you have mechanical skills would be buying vintage sports cars. There is a current trend, especially in the baby boomer generation, towards muscle cars and older convertible sports cars. These men and women are reaching their 50's and 60's and have extra money to enjoy a classic sports car. The allure of high performance engines, the smell of softened leather or the magic of a convertible top down on a moonlit night are all reasons for the popularity of sports cars. Car buffs who are into sports cars seem to look the other way at inflation. If they want a 1956 Astin Martin DB4 convertible and there were only 215 made, the price for one at $200,000 is meaningless, they tell their friends, "I just got to have that Astin Martin DB4 sports car, and it fits my personality!"

I have a story to share of a friend on mine, who I partnered with as a vendor resource when I worked at Commercial 35 – a 35mm slide production lab. Bruce was into cars. He enjoyed them immensely and had the mechanical skills to match. He researched some Porsche race cars and finally found a 1966 Porsche race car that needed restoration. The factory only made 65 of them when they were built. He bought the car "as is" for $11,000 in 1974 at age 31, and worked three years in his spare time restoring the car completely. Bruce's plan was to tuck the car in his father's garage and let it sit for the next 20 plus years and then sell the car for a profit to have extra money for retirement. I called Bruce when I was doing my book research to have him share his story. He sold the car in 2000 and was paid $250,000 for his 1966 restored Porsche race car. He has since been using the money investing in mutual funds and some for part of his monthly living expenses. Bruce also shared with me that back in the 1960's you could have bought a Porsche 356 Speedster (common sports car of the day) for around $3,000. Today those same sports cars in great condition are selling for between $60,000 to $80,000. So do your homework, spend time carefully searching for the right car, buy as low as you can, restore where needed and garage the car for years to come and then sell it when you can secure the price you want.

Here is a list of sports car makers you can draw upon ranging in years 1945 to 1990:

-Alfa Romeo	-Allard	-Aston Martin
-Austin Healey	-Bugatti	-BMW
-Cadillac	-Cobra	-Chevy Corvette
-Corvair	-Delorean	-Dodge Charger
-Dodge Stealth	-Dodge Viper	-Excaliber
-Ferrari	-Fiat	-Ford Mustang
-Honda	-Jaguar	-Lamborghini
-Lotus	-Maserati	-Mazda
-Mercedes Benz	-MG	-Nissan
-Panther	-Porsche	-Toyota
-Triumph	-Volkswagen	-Volvo

Summary

I have shared only a couple of ideas for looking at income diversification. Hopefully I have planted the seeds for your success in this area. Use your talents to the best of your ability, invest your time wisely and hopefully make some extra money for yourself. If you are skilled with reading or math abilities, become a tutor to children who need extra help in that area. There are many parents now days that are willing to pay $10.00 to $25.00 an hour for tutoring their child to keep ahead in school programs. Teach music lessons one to two evenings a week for extra income. I'm also thinking if you have talent with soccer or baseball or swimming, talk to youth leagues and coaches to discover if any parents are willing to pay for private sports lessons for their son or daughter. You would be amazed at what parents will spend on their children to advance a sport.

The world awaits you in this area. Don't be afraid to step out and try different hobbies or new applications in your life. By viewing less TV and Internet hours, you can make a huge impact on your future by spending "quality" hours investing in your future.

9

SUMMARY

My main goal and desire in writing this book was to guide and assist young adults in realizing their potential in life **"sooner versus later"** so that I could help pave their pathways sharper, clearer, faster and stronger. The book was designed as a resource guide to gain wisdom and insight as to better forecasting your future. The information you acquire from reading each chapter and absorbing the knowledge should prepare you to be a more successful adult at an earlier age. But don't just read the material and not **apply it**! You have to fuel the fire, **be a doer** and not a reader only. What I have learned in my life the past fifty years is that **WISDOM** becomes a key principle to living longer, being happy and finding your own personal basis for financial gratitude. The more knowledgeable about a subject, the better prepared you become. Every individual will achieve their own success levels. A person who decides to become a doctor, after completing 4 years of undergraduate school, 4 years of medical school and 3 to 7 years of residency training, will finally succeed by reaching the end of their goal as a physician. But, that person paid a dedicated price, attending 11 to 15 years of schooling and heaps of student loans. As they transition onto their next life stage, success begins to snowball. The person who attends a trade school, and graduates to become a beautician or mechanic, will secure a job making an income and find their success attainment. We all can experience success at the different levels, which we achieve for ourselves. Happiness, joy, money, secure job, it all relates to the pathways we choose in life. What you make of life is up to you! You pave your own roadway. Interstate highways are not built in a month. They take years of engineering, planning, budgeting, financing, deciding the right construction company, and building the road...one mile at a time.

When you procure your first job, here is a strategy plan I suggest you follow. As soon as you qualify for participating in the company 401K plan start investing in the program. Most companies offer matching funds to encourage your participation. Invest your money to the maximum dollar that your employer matches. For every dollar you put in they offer matching funds up to X amount dollars per month.

After you have full dollar matching in your company 401K, start diverting your money. First, if you are in debt, start taking your extra money to pay down on that debt. Why? Because paying down your balances on your credit cards will lower your debt to credit ratio figures, and allow your FICO score numbers to climb higher. Elevated FICO scores mean lower interest rates, better deals and offerings on loans.

If you are not loaded with credit card debt then go to the next step.

Buy your first house! Start saving money toward a down payment. Depending upon your individual circumstances, you many qualify with no money down or try to negotiate a 5-20% down payment to purchase a house. There are a lot of options here (see chapter 5 on buying your first house). In most cases if you can, work to save toward a 10% down payment. Here's why I think buying a house is so important. For my example I will keep it simple and use the purchase of a $100,000 home. You put a $10,000 down payment on the house and borrow the rest. Keep in mind that homes in the St. Louis marketplace have been appreciating 5% to 10% the past 5 years. So let's assume a modest 5% increase in appreciation value the first year. On your $10,000 investment in a home, after one year you made a $5,000 return (house appreciation value after one year is $105,000) or a 50% rate of return on your $10,000 investment. Folks, you can hardly do that these days in the stock market, gold, diamonds, or anywhere else.

So work extra hard to save your money and invest in the purchase of a home as soon as you can! Real estate is a solid, and strong empowerment that appreciates in value.

Next step, start an investment program with a professional financial planner. The earlier you start investing the better off you will be in your retirement years. There are two other areas to be keenly aware of at this stage. If you believe in college, and someday plan to have a family, now might be a good time to start a college fund for your children.

The other goal would be to buy some kind of life insurance program. I recommend starting out with some term insurance, weighing the monthly cost as to how much you can afford, and the proper amount for your lifestyle.

A quick recap for a solid game plan to direct your money upon starting that first job:

1. Invest money in your company 401K plan to the maximum matching employer funds.
2. Direct your money to paying off any debts you have accrued.
3. Buy a house, the investment and appreciation in real estate is key growth potential.
4. Start an investment program with a professional financial planner.
5. Buy some life insurance and maybe look at starting a college fund for your children.

You can do anything you desire to do! Recognize there is the principle of seed, time, and harvest. Plot your course with careful thought and precise planning. When I sat down in my "quiet time" period one day and decided I would write a book to help guide pathways for young adults, my goal was to share principles I did not know about or understand when I was twenty five years old. A seed was planted, goals were set in motion and written down. Time was spent doing research and writing page upon page, until after almost two years, I had a printed book. Now, I am coming closer to my harvest of filling a need for information to young adults who I care very much about. What are your plans, pursuits and purposes for your life? Plant your seeds carefully and wisely while you are young so you can reap a fuller harvest for yourself in later years.

Three of the biggest decisions you will make upon leaving High School include:

1. Choosing the right career path for you personally.
2. Choosing the right mate to marry.
3. Choosing the right first house to buy.

I can't make those decisions for you. I can't guarantee your success or happiness in life. But with the information in this book I can guide you to achieving a higher success ratio for your roadmap in life. I challenge you to strive to work toward the complete package. Every chapter contains portions of the pie to assist you to be a winner and not a loser.

Let's review the pie chart:

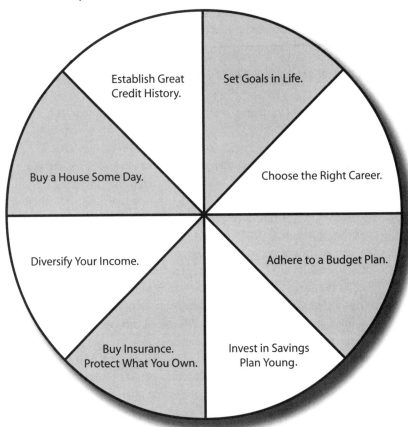

By applying the portions of the pie in the right stages of you life I know you can be better prepared than I was. That's what this book is all about, helping you know more, so you can grow more...and be able to run faster, jump higher, climb over the hurdles in life to achieve the best person you can be! Go for it! And enjoy the rideeeeeeeeeeeeeee eeeeeeeeeeeeeeeee!

My final thoughts on living a long, happy, healthy, and prosperous life:
- Exercise on a regular basis.
- Choose carefully the people you associate with.
- Watch the foods you eat.
- Develop a better understanding of diet, good foods versus bad foods.

- Take the right vitamins you need for your body on a daily basis.
- Drink a lot of water on a daily basis.
- Don't make rash and quick decisions, take time to think about it.
- Take at least one week of vacation every year, get away to clear out the cobwebs.
- Attend Church on a regular basis.
- Be a giver, help people where ever you can.
- Become a reader, read for pleasure, knowledge and increased learning.
- Give 3 compliments a day to people.
- Learn to bury the past (forget about your mistakes and move on) before it buries you.
- Invest in yourself and start saving money in your mid-twenties.
- Limit the television and/or Internet hours you view daily.
- Constantly work on expanding and growing your God given talents.
- **Smile...be happy, don't WORRY!**

BIOGRAPHY

John Wesley Eyres was born in St. Louis, Missouri, in 1954. He spent the first years of his life in North St. Louis (learning city skills), attending Bel-Nor Grade School and Normandy Jr. High. Then in the eighth grade John's parents moved to De Soto, Missouri, buying 20 acres of woodland property with a lake. John enjoyed a country lifestyle, graduating from Hillsboro High School in 1973.

He attended Jefferson Junior College, in Hillsboro, Missouri on a two-year music scholarship program and then transferred to Central Missouri State College, in Warrensburg, Missouri, graduating with a B.M.E. in 1977. John taught music as a band director to grades 5 through 12, for two years at Adrian R-3 Schools, 45 miles south of Kansas City, Missouri.

Desiring to move back home to St. Louis and establish his roots, John changed careers and took a photography copy-stand job at Commercial 35, Inc. in the summer of 1979. After learning the 35mm slide production business from the inside out for five years, he was promoted to an account sales position. Here, he found a niche area of work that he enjoyed and stayed in sales. His sales background included Audio Visual Rentals, Advertising, Business Disaster Recovery Services, Computer Rentals, the Mortgage industry, Video Production and he is currently working in the IT and Facilities Management field.

John is married to Kristine L. Eyres, who has been a dental hygienist for over 28 years. They celebrated their 25th wedding anniversary in November of 2004. They have four children; Whitney, Blake, McKenzie, and Gabrielle. They currently reside in Creve Coeur, Missouri and attend Faith Christian Ministries Church, where they have been members for over 20 years.

NOTES:

_____

_____

_____

_____

_____

_____

_____

_____

_____

_____

_____

_____

_____

_____

_____

_____

_____

_____

_____

_____

_____

_____

_____

_____

_____

I WANT TO HEAR FROM YOU

If you have a comment or would like to share how this book has helped you, I would like to hear from you. Please feel free to write me or contact me online at my web site.

If you would like to purchase this book for a friend just go online to the web site and order your copy of **Showin' Ya The Ropes.**

To contact me in writing, mail to:

John Eyres
12713 Willowyck Drive
St. Louis, MO 63146

To contact me to be a public speaker at your next school function, meeting, or event go online to the web site and select Public Speaking Request.

Please tell your friends to visit my web site at:

(ShowinYaTheRopes.com)